# LIVING LIFE [*inside*] THE LINES

# MARTHA SIGALL

UNIVERSITY PRESS OF MISSISSIPPI

*JACKSON*

# LIVING LIFE [ *inside* ] THE LINES

TALES FROM

THE GOLDEN AGE

OF ANIMATION

www.upress.state.ms.us

Designed by Todd Lape

The University Press of Mississippi is a member of the
Association of American University Presses.

Illustrations on pages ii, iii, v, and vi from the model
sheet of Sniffles, © Warner Bros. Entertainment, Inc.
Courtesy of Jerry Beck.

First edition 2005

∞

Library of Congress Cataloging-in-Publication Data

Sigall, Martha.
 Living life inside the lines : tales from the golden age of
animation / Martha Sigall.—1st ed.
    p. cm.
 Includes index.
 ISBN 1-57806-748-0 (cloth : alk. paper) —
 ISBN 1-57806-749-9 (pbk. : alk. paper)
   1. Animated films—California—Los Angeles—History
and criticism. 2. Sigall, Martha. 3. Hollywood (Los Angeles, Calif.)—Biography. 4. Los Angeles (Calif.)—Biography. I. Title.
 NC1766.U5S54 2005
 741.5'8'092—dc22                          2004022897

British Library Cataloging-in-Publication Data available

To
My husband, Sol,
Our sons, Bob and Lee,
Their wives, Lei and Eve,
Our grandchildren, Nicole and Dustin,
And, all the future generations to come

# [ *contents* ]

# [ *foreword* ]

One day, sometime back in 1992, I got a call from Martha Sigall. That was how we met. She just called me out of the blue.

I don't remember the specifics of our conversation, but I'm always happy to talk to any Warner Bros. cartoon fan, especially if I have a few minutes to answer a simple question about Looney Tunes and Merrie Melodies.

I had just spent over fifteen years researching the histories of the Hollywood cartoons, as research assistant to Leonard Maltin on his landmark book *Of Mice and Magic*, as coauthor (with Will Friedwald) of *The Warner Bros. Cartoons* and a revised edition called *Looney Tunes and Merrie Melodies: A Complete Illustrated Guide to the Warner Bros. Cartoons*, and as sole author of a tribute to Tweety and Sylvester entitled *I Tawt I Taw a Puddy Tat*. The Warner Bros. cartoons are my favorite films of all time and have given me inspiration for every aspect of my life.

Apparently, Martha had figured out I lived in Los Angeles and decided to call instead of write. As I said, I don't recall the specifics, but I do remember one thing she said: that she had collected all of the Warner cartoons on tape, except for an elusive one hundred or so.

That meant she had over nine hundred Warner Bros. cartoons on video. I'd never heard of anyone collecting the whole set that way. They weren't released officially on video—and I certainly didn't have such personal access to the cartoons myself. I liked the idea of knowing someone who did.

So, for purely selfish reasons, I decided to help Martha complete her collection. That way, if for some research purpose, I needed to see any of them, I could get a copy from Martha without having to borrow from a group of private film collectors I knew or the Warner Bros. archives themselves.

Within the next month or so, we completed her collection (now she had over one thousand cartoons from 1930 to 1969) but, even better, I got to meet and know Martha and her husband, Sol. Since then, we've become more than friends. I've felt like their adopted son—a member of the family.

The coolest thing about Martha is that she was part of it all. She was there, at Leon Schlesinger's studio and later at the MGM animation unit. She was friends with Chuck Jones, Bob Clampett, Tex Avery, Bill Hanna, Joe Barbera, Friz Freleng, Frank Tashlin, Michael Maltese, and on and on.

These were names I revered. Some I got to meet in their later years, some I only know and admire from their work on screen. Martha knew them personally, and she had worked right alongside them. I had guessed right—those guys (and gals) had a ball making those cartoons.

Martha started as a teenager as a painter and then inker in what we now refer to as the golden age of animation, and she has lived to see some of her coworkers become latter-day celebrities, recognized for talents that were generally ignored at the time. Unlike some of her colleagues who dismissed their work on cartoons as things of the past, Martha still watched the cartoons and became quite an expert on them.

Over the years, we have had numerous brunches, dinners (ahh, the Cheesecake Factory), and phone calls, and Martha never hesitated to answer my most trivial questions.

Thankfully, she has now put all of her memories of those days in animation down in this book. Her story is an important historical document. She was a backstage eyewitness to the evolution of one of the twentieth century's greatest art forms and a first-hand observer and participant in the making of the world's funniest and most popular cartoons.

I am grateful that Martha's book enlightens us on the inner workings of Termite Terrace. Her point of view shows us the Looney Tunes

from another perspective, not from a supervising director or animation artist but from the work-a-day world all of us can relate to.

I'd give anything to trade places with Martha and to have been
there myself, but this book is the next best thing. I know you will
enjoy it as much as I have.

Well, I should stop talking and let Martha begin.

That's all, folks!

**—JERRY BECK**

# [ *acknowledgments* ]

First of all, I want to thank my husband, Sol, for his support and help during every phase of this book including research, viewing cartoons, and the typing of every word into our computer; and our sons, Bob and Lee, who urged me to write my remembrances of my days in animation, if only for the benefit of our family.

I must admit that I did not relent, though, until our good friend, Jerry Beck, a well-published author and animation historian, insisted that I needed to do this for, as he put it, "Martha, there should be some way of preserving you."

My thanks also go to the following:

Leith Adams, the head archivist at the Warner Bros. Museum, who read my first draft and has helped me every step of the way since.

Mark Kausler, whose fund of knowledge about the animation industry is gigantic and who is always willing to share that knowledge.

Bob Casino, who knows everything about the MGM Cartoon Studio and helped so much to jog my memory about my years there.

Paula and Jim Faris for their help with the MGM years.

Michael Mallory for his cogent thoughts.

Evelyn Wood, a fellow docent at the Warner Bros. Museum and a published author, who offered so many helpful ideas.

Kathy Merlock Jackson, professor and chair of communications at Virginia Wesleyan College, for her very valid suggestions and glowing report.

Julie Heath of Warner Bros. Clips-Stills Licensing Department for her invaluable help.

And all the wonderful people with whom I worked at all the studios who really made this book possible. My feelings for all of you go far beyond the few words on this page.

# [ *introduction* ]

These stories and events are some of the things that went on during the years I worked in the animated cartoon business. To me, it was a really fun business. The people were, for the most part, so wonderful, fun loving, and young, and they were always playing gags and tricks on one another. The very nature of the business produced these types of people.

I started with Leon Schlesinger Productions, producer of Looney Tunes and Merrie Melodies. The date was July 13, 1936, which, today, is considered part of the golden age of animation.

Even though I started as an apprentice painter for just $12.75 a week, and a forty-four-hour week at that, I considered myself very lucky to be working there. It was so much fun that, when I woke up in the morning, I couldn't wait to get to work for I knew it would be another fun day and I couldn't wait to see what would happen. Even though we did have fun, we still got our work done. You can see from all the times I've used the word "fun," it really must have been just that—fun.

The people were so great. Many of them became our lifelong friends, people like Shirley and (Dave) Milton Kahn, Juliet and Herman Cohen, Dixie and Paul Smith, Florrie and Mike Maltese, Lola and Lew Irwin, Peggi and Bob Matz, and Eleanor and Larry Silverman. Whenever we got together, within five minutes, we would start reminiscing about the stories that happened in the "olden days."

I have tried to recapture what it was like to work in an animation studio in those early days. What I have written is my own recollection of what happened on a day-to-day basis and of the people who made those things happen. Some of these stories I consider classics and they should not be lost. I'm sure I can't remember all of them, but while there are some remaining in my memory, here they are. I hope you enjoy them.

# LIVING LIFE [*inside*] THE LINES

# [ *chapter 1* ]

# THE BEGINNING, 1932

When people find out that I worked in animation, their faces light up, their eyes get wide, and they ask me, "How did you ever get into such an exciting business?" I generally answer, "Just lucky, I guess, and being in the right place at the right time—twice." With wider eyes and their interest piqued, they ask me to explain. So. . . .

Just before I was to be enrolled at Le Conte Junior High School on Bronson Avenue in Hollywood, California, my family moved to a house at 1128 Tamarind Avenue. That was being in the right place the first time. We soon discovered that, in the house directly behind us, on Bronson Avenue, lived a very nice family by the name of Wanlass: Ewell and Verda, and their four daughters, with whom I played. We took a wood slat from the fence so that we could go back and forth to each other's home instead of going all the way around the block.

The property consisted of four buildings, two facing the street, one behind the main office and which housed the lab, and the other occupied by the Wanlass family. It was all owned by Pacific Title and Art Studio and was the original location of the now well-known company then owned by Leon Schlesinger. In these early days, Pacific Title was one of the few companies that produced titles for the silent feature films. With the advent of sound, Pacific Titles' business decreased since there was no further need for the dialogue cards, but they did continue to produce the main titles and the lists of screen credits.

The right front building was actually a five-room residential house, but it was occupied by a few people working as artists and by Larry Glickman, the manager, who later became the owner.

The left front building housed the main office. Its front looked like a Swiss chalet, very unusual for a commercial business. The large front room was occupied by Jack Stevens, whose job it was to print some of the titles on black cards. A few years later, he worked at Leon Schlesinger's cartoon studio as the night cameraman. Several years after that, Jack worked as the head cameraman at MGM Cartoons.

Jack's brother, Hank ("Smokey") Garner, did odd jobs and could fix anything mechanical. He also made the move to Leon Schlesinger's as the studio projectionist and shot the animators' drawings on a pencil test camera he had rigged up.

Mr. Schlesinger's office was in this building as was George Larson's, the bookkeeper.

Many different film companies shot scenes in front of the office building because of its unique front. Although this happened several times, only one stands out in my memory, probably because it was a kids' movie and had a lot of child actors. In this *Mickey Maguire* film, the lead was a nine-year-old boy who played a tough little kid, wore a black derby, vest, and pants, and had a rubber cigar dangling from the corner of his mouth. At the time, he went by the stage name of Mickey Maguire, but when he grew up, he became that terrifically talented actor Mickey Rooney. Golly, now that I look back on it, it was definitely exciting living in Hollywood during those days.

Directly behind the main office was a film lab where newsreels were developed. Ewell Wanlass was the foreman of that lab, and he rented the rear house from Leon.

Ewell's daughter Beth would take me into the building adjacent to the main office, a building occupied by Larry Glickman, Hal Porter, an artist, and the only woman to work there, Thelma, whose last name I never knew. Thelma worked in the front room and had two desks. One had a large easel with a large air compressor next to it, where she did all the airbrushing on the titles. When she didn't have any airbrushing to do, she moved to the second desk where she painted animation.

Even though it was interesting to watch her using the airbrush, something I had never seen before, it was more exciting to me to see her paint cartoon characters like Bosko, Honey, and Bruno. I had seen those charactors in all the movie theatres, but I had no idea how they were made. So that she would have no objection to my watching, I tried to make myself as useful as I could to her. I washed out her paint jars and refilled them with clean water and I cleaned her paint brushes. As she got to know me better, she had me clean unwanted smudges from her work.

Every paper drawing was matched by a celluloid sheet of the same size. These were called "cels." The animator's paper drawings were numbered and then traced on to the cel in India ink by pen, including the number. This was done to keep the cels in proper sequence.

Thelma painted the cels for Mr. Schlesinger, who was also the producer of the Merrie Melodies and Looney Tunes cartoons distributed by Warner Bros.

These cartoons were directed by Hugh Harman and Rudy Ising at the Harman-Ising Studio on Hollywood Boulevard near Wilton Place.

A scene from one of the cartoons was sent to Thelma to paint. At that time, all the scenes were painted in black, white, and gray colors. She had a variety of those colors on the top of her second desk. Also on this desk was a gooseneck lamp and several long rows of shelves on which she placed the painted cels as she finished each color. Each cel was painted with one color and then put on the shelf to dry as Thelma applied the paint to the next cel. Usually by the time she finished the last cel, the first cel was dry enough for her to apply the second color, and so on.

The employees in all the buildings would have a "break" at the same time each afternoon. One day I was standing around the lot eating a candy bar when one of the fellows asked, "Hey, kid, can you get me one of those candy bars?" I said, "Sure," and he gave me a nickel to get one for him. And, off I went to get it.

Word spread to the others, and they all began asking me to get them a snack, too. There were no such things as catering trucks at that time. I became a "gofer" to get ice cream, candy, sodas, and other miscellaneous goodies for them.

Equipped with my brother Allan's new red wagon, I collected nickels, dimes, and quarters, and, beaming with my newly acquired sense of purpose, I hurried to the nearby confectionary to fill their orders. At the end of the week, they all gave me a tip of five or ten cents. George Larson always gave me a quarter. This turned my Fridays into "pay days," which amounted to a dollar and a half or two dollars. Every penny counted during those days of the Great Depression, and I considered this a meaningful sum. I proudly added these earnings to the family budget, helping to buy food and pay bills for the next three years. My parents were so proud of me!

By the summer of 1932, I had graduated from junior high school, but I was still running errands and helping Thelma. When I had no chores, I watched as she painted. She was so careful to stay within the lines. One day, she became ill and had to leave work early. Her instructions to me were, "When the cels are dry, please clean them and put them in numerical order. The messenger will come to pick up the work. Most of the scene is finished, but there are twenty that still need one color. Tell them that I am really sorry." When she left, I could tell she was very upset. I assured her I would take care of it. Although watching paint dry is not universally known as motivating, it proved so to me. As I leaned over the wet cels, inspiration struck! I could finish the scene! The white paint jar was still open on her desk. It was just a matter of painting the eyes, collars, and gloves. After all, hadn't I seen her do this over and over again for the past three years? My confidence soared knowing she would not have to be upset about leaving her work unfinished if I could complete the job!

Thelma had always been so nice to me. It only seemed right to help her out when she needed it most.

I slipped into her little white gloves, worn by everyone who touches cels, and picked up her brush. Of course, the entire time that I was painting her work, my heart was pounding because, down deep, I knew I was doing something I was really not supposed to do. But my youthful zeal wouldn't let me stop until I finished those twenty cels.

I noticed it was almost time for the fellows to go on their break. I rushed home to get Allan's wagon and waited for the men to come outside. After I filled their orders, I rushed back to Thelma's desk to see if the work was dry. Luckily, it was. I looked it over and it seemed fine. I cleaned the cels, put them in numerical order, and checked the work again just to make sure.

When the messenger came, I handed him the scene without saying anything but I was sure he could hear my heart pounding. I picked up Allan's wagon and went home.

My mother sensed something different about me. She asked, "Is everything all right?" My guilty look must have been showing. I usually told her everything, but I was afraid she would bawl me out for what I had done. So, I said nothing about it and changed the subject. But try as I might, I just couldn't help thinking about it.

As the hours passed, my confidence sank lower and lower. What if I had done something wrong? I did check it and re-check it, I tried to reassure myself. I kept debating in my mind and trying to convince myself it had to be o.k. These thoughts kept me awake most of the night. Then I realized I would have to tell Thelma the next morning what I had done. I was so mad at myself for not doing only what she had told me.

The next morning, I was waiting for her. I didn't know if she would be out sick. I was standing out on the sidewalk when I saw her get off the streetcar at Santa Monica Boulevard. I stood frozen in my tracks as she walked up the street. I waited until she was within a few feet of me and then blurted out what I had done.

Over a half century has passed since that day, but I can still picture the color draining from her face! She exclaimed, "Oh, my gosh, why did you do that? I'll be in all kinds of trouble if anything is wrong." My heart sank to the pit of my stomach.

Thelma wasted no time in calling the Harman-Ising Studio telling them what had happened. She was reassured by the person on the other end of the line that the entire scene was o.k. She was told the camera department needed that scene and actually had already shot it.

Whew! The weight of the world was lifted from my shoulders, and she was, understandably, relieved. But she made me promise I would never do anything like that again. It didn't occur to me back then but, today, as an adult, I can visualize how I would react if a teenager had finished one of my scenes.

At ten o'clock that morning, as was his habit, Mr. Schlesinger, dressed to the "nines" in a fashionable suit, shirt, and tie, a carnation always tucked into the buttonhole of his jacket, drove up in his Cadillac. Instead of going directly to his office, he made his way up the steps to Thelma's room. The fragrance of his Yardley cologne had announced his arrival before he came into view.

Entering the room, he nudged Thelma as he looked toward me, "Is this the kid who finished your scene?" She admitted that I was the guilty party and quickly added that I had vowed never to take that liberty again. Mr. Schlesinger's response to her was, "That's all right. Show her how to do the work." Then, looking back at me, he added, "Study art in school, Martha, and I'll give you a job in my cartoon studio when you graduate." Relieved that he wasn't angry and delighted that he made this generous offer, I thanked him profusely.

For the rest of my summer vacation, I continued to run errands for the fellows and to help Thelma, but this wasn't all I did. I chummed around with my two best friends, Rhoda Chasman and Louise Kaslow, who are still close friends of mine today. I played softball with the neighborhood kids. When we chose up sides for the two teams, I was always selected first. And, boy, did the fellows hate that! I was a good baseball player in those days. All of us made scooters using orange crates nailed to a 2 x 4 board to which we added roller skate wheels. I also had to do chores around the house.

Soon I was back in high school and involved with my studies, homework, and school activities to the extent that I forgot all about the cartoon business.

I found out that Mr. Schlesinger had sold Pacific Title to his manager, Larry Glickman. Thelma no longer painted the Looney Tune cels, and I no longer ran errands for the people working there.

On the afternoon of March 10, 1933, a bunch of us were playing softball on the playground at Le Conte Junior High when one of the boys, Jimmy Morris, said, "Let's go home, gang. There's going to be an earthquake." So, like good little sheep, all of us went home.

Upon my arrival at home, my mother said, "I'm glad you're home. I have dinner ready." The talk about the earthquake had already slipped my mind. We sat down to dinner, but before we could even start eating, we heard the most horrific sounding roar, a sound I can't possibly describe but one I never forgot. This was followed by tremendous shaking. Items were falling from our shelves. Our family ran out of the house and into the Wanlass family yard. They were out there, too, as well as all the people from Pacific Title. As we stood there, we could feel the ground going up and down. What a vibration! This sensation made my knees weak!

After about ten minutes, my mother suggested going back into the house. Only one thing was broken—my brother's ceramic Mickey Mouse. Throughout the evening, there were many aftershocks, and each time this happened, I felt my knees get weak. We listened to the radio all that evening. We heard that most of the damage was centered in the city of Long Beach and the surrounding areas.

The next day, the newspapers were full of pictures and news reports. The devastation seemed to center on brick buildings, schools, and hospitals. The worst news concerned the loss of life and serious injuries.

The final results were that the earthquake was of the magnitude 6.4, which resulted in 120 deaths and fifty million dollars in property damage.

All through the earthquake and aftershocks, I kept thinking about what Jimmy had said. I couldn't wait to see him the next day. Everyone was asking him how he knew there was going to be an earthquake. He shrugged and said he didn't know what made him say that!

On Monday morning, when I arrived at Hollywood High School, I could see that the Administration Building looked out of kilter. Ropes and barriers were all around the building with a sign that said the structure had been condemned.

Although students were not allowed to go into the building, many of us had our lockers there. For a very short time, the teachers were allowed to go in to bring out our books and anything else we had in our lockers.

My Latin class with Esther Abbott was changed from that building to the football field.

Our Hollywood area seemed to recover quickly and life went on. It was still deep depression time and people were more concerned making ends meet, putting food on the table, and paying their rent. Two very ordinary years passed and soon I was a senior at Hollywood High.

In that year, we moved about five blocks away. I was grown up by then and I was hoping to go to college. But, after graduation, since my parents weren't able to send me for more schooling, not even junior college, I went looking for work, but to no avail. These were still depression days and jobs were still very difficult to find in any field. I did work in sales in the five and ten cents store for a few days, but that was not regular work. It was really no job.

Since jobs did not appear to be available in Hollywood, I usually concentrated on downtown Los Angeles because there were so many more businesses. This, in itself, did not mean that I would secure a position there—and I didn't, but I did keep trying.

My transportation was the bus or the streetcar. On this fateful day, I was headed back to Hollywood, but I missed the bus and took the streetcar instead. This meant that instead of getting off at Sunset and walking down a block to my friend Kas's house, for that's where I was heading, I took the streetcar and got off at Santa Monica and Van Ness and walked up Van Ness for four blocks to her home. What a difference that made!

As I was walking up Van Ness, at the corner of Van Ness and Fern-wood, whom did I see but Mr. Schlesinger. He was watching men who were painting "Leon Schlesinger Productions, Producer of Merrie Melodies and Looney Tunes" on the side of a building, the old building that Warner Bros. had vacated around 1929.

All of a sudden, everything came back to me. I remembered his promise to give me a job in his cartoon studio. So I hurried over to him and said, "Hello, Mr. Schlesinger, do you remember me?" He looked at me and said, "No, I can't say that I do." I told him, "I'm Martha Goldman." "Do you mean that you're that little kid who used to run around the studio lot in jeans?" "That's me," I replied, "but I'm all grown up now and need a job." He said, "Did you study art in school?" "Yes," I lied. He said, "Well, I'll tell you. We are on vacation right now, but are going back to work on July 13. You come to the studio on that morning and I will give you a job. We start work at 8 A.M. I suggest that you arrive between 7:30 and 7:45." That was being in the right place for the second time.

That's the way I got into the business. The year was 1936. My employee's card, which I still have, will verify that date. All together, I was in animation over fifty-three years. During that time, I worked for just about every cartoon studio in existence then, with the exception of Disney. However, I did work on Disney cartoons when they faced a deadline and had to farm work out to some of the ink and paint studios that I worked for.

# [ *chapter 2* ]

# MY FIRST DAY
# IN ANIMATION

My first day at Schlesinger's, July 13, 1936, I was at the studio bright and early. A blonde woman sat on the bench in the lobby. She smiled and told me her name, "Gladys Hallberg." I introduced myself and we had a brief conversation. Another young woman came in who was also new and reporting for work. Her name was Mary Lane.

A man came out of the office and told us he was Henry Binder, who, we were to find out, was the office manager. He said that he would take us up to the ink and paint department as soon as we filled out applications. When that was done, Mr. Binder took us upstairs and introduced us to Art Goble, the supervisor, and Betty Brenon, his assistant. Art found desks for the three of us. I was seated between two experienced painters, Betty Hielborn and Sylvia Rogers.

I noticed rows and rows of desks, all of which had gooseneck lamps like the type Thelma had used. Just as Thelma was set up, rows of shelves were behind the lamp, shelves on which to place the wet cels.

Dozens of young women were standing around talking. Their lighthearted conversations regarding their just-completed vacations were suddenly stopped by the ringing of the bell. Everyone went to

Employee's card from 1936. Later, in 1942, because the employees of Leon Schlesinger Productions would be working on classified training films for the U.S. armed forces, an identity card was issued to each of them. These cards had to be worn throughout the duration of World War II. Elements under copyright of Warner Bros. Entertainment, Inc.

her desk and started to work. It soon became so quiet. While I sat there, I grew more nervous at the prospect of not being able to succeed at this new and exciting job. I didn't know if these women would accept me—I was so young compared to them. But the main thing on my mind was, could I learn to paint? It looked so easy when Thelma did it. I told myself that at least I was familiar with the types of materials and equipment that were to be used. Before I could get too nervous and worried, Betty Brenon brought me work. Sitting down beside me, she painted the first few cels. First of all, it was just eyes. She gave me about thirty cels to do. There was nothing else on the cels, just eyes. Betty said, "Let me see you do one." I did it, apparently to her satisfaction, for she then said, "That's good. Now, do the rest of them and when you finish, show them to me." That's what I did. Since I was just doing eyes, you might say that these cels might be considered "limited animation," using a blank face on a cel that would be held in place with just the eyes animating on separate cels.

Signage on the wall outside of Leon Schlesinger Productions on Van Ness and Wilton in Hollywood. © Warner Bros. Entertainment, Inc. Courtesy of Jerry Beck.

The cels with the eyes would be overlaid on to the cel with the blank face. We did things like that in those early years.

After I finished those thirty cels, I showed them to Betty, who said, "Fine, now I want you to paint the rest of the scene. I want you to paint all that you see that is color identified. Everything is marked for you." The color model sheet that she handed me showed the characters that were on the cels with every part of those characters marked with the color that was to be put on and with the proper place marked with a line that ran from that place to the color indicated. Betty said, "I want you to do the white first. When finished, show it to me." I did the white and showed it to her. Each time I finished a color, I had to show it to her. "This is the way that I want you to get used to painting," she said. The whole scene was about three hundred cels, and it took me almost ten days to do.

The cartoon, "At Your Service, Madame," features a mama pig, Mrs. Hamhocks, and her six little piglets. Also featured is W.C. Squeals, a caricature of W.C. Fields, complete with his mannerisms,

Former Schlesinger cartoon studio as it is today, boarded up and part of television station KTLA. Martha Goldman Sigall Collection.

looks, and voice. He reads in the *Daily Bugle* that Mrs. Hamhocks, a widow, has inherited a fortune. He wastes no time calling on her. Upon being invited in, he proceeds to flatter her by calling her "my little chickadee," and he compliments her on her lovely home.

As he scans the room, he notices a safe built into the wall next to her piano. As though he has x-ray vision, he fantasizes about all the money in that safe. He suggests that she play while he sings. He stands next to the piano and sings "At Your Service, Madame" while, at the same time, eyeing her safe.

One of the little piglets, curious to see what is happening, stands behind W.C. and looks up at him. W.C. tells him, "Run along, son, you bother me." When the piglet refuses to budge, W.C. pushes and kicks him away. This is enough for the piglet to know that something is wrong. He gathers his brothers together to discuss a potentially bad situation.

"AT YOUR SERVICE MADAME"
Merrie Melodie #12

"At Your Service, Madame." Model sheet of W.C. Squeals from this cartoon directed by Friz Fre-leng, animated by Cal Dalton and Don Williams, musical direction by Norman Spencer—and the first cartoon on which the author painted. © Warner Bros. Entertainment, Inc. Martha Gold-man Sigall Collection.

Meanwhile, W.C. Squeals has opened the safe and is filling his pockets with the money. Next, we see a piglet carrying a light socket attached to an electrical cord which is plugged into a lamp. The socket is attached to W.C.'s tail and another piglet turns on the switch.

Now comes my scene: W.C. is shocked, sparks fly all over the place as he screams and yells. Part of the same scene, but not my section, shows Mama pig, who is still unaware that she has been robbed, bawling out her son for his mischief. Back to my section: two other piglets who are upstairs lower a rope that has a big hook on the end of it. They swing the rope and catch the hook on the tail of W.C.'s coat. He is lifted up and swung back and forth until he flies right into the living room window where another piglet is waiting and slams the window down on his neck. End of my section. Two more piglets bring in a reducing machine, and the belt is wrapped around W.C.'s body and the machine turned on. All of the money is shaken out of his coat.

Mama now realizes what has transpired and hugs all her little off-spring. W.C. Squeals is ejected from the window and lands on the ground. He picks himself up, still shaking as he walks away, and the cartoon ends.

I did one other small scene in that cartoon: the little piglet with the red bow tie comes into the living room and grabs one of the curtains. That scene took only half a day.

I suppose that it's because these scenes were the very first I worked on and also because I have seen this cartoon a number of times that I remember it so well. I have seen many others that I worked on but cannot remember the exact scenes that I did. Because I actually counted them, I know that I worked on 200 of the 250 cartoons that were produced during the seven years I was at Schlesinger's. I missed out on the other 50 because they were produced by the Ray Katz unit and directed by Bob Clampett.

The studio always screened the cartoons for the employees when a picture was finished and I couldn't wait to see the first one I had worked on. After I was there about a month, "At Your Service, Madame," my very first picture, was shown. I was so nervous! I was so excited! To think that work I had done on a cartoon would be shown all across the country and, maybe, even most of the world! I knew that only my family and some of my friends would know about my participation, that only they would recognize the scene I had done, for, of course, I would have already described it to each of them. The part that I had spent ten days on went by so fast on the screen. It went by in a flash. Twenty-four frames go by in one second! Usually, the action is planned so that each cel is exposed twice, which makes the animation smoother. This means that, usually, it takes twelve cels for each second.

In the early days of animation, a six- or seven-minute cartoon consisted of about ten thousand drawings and took about nine months to produce from the start of the storyboard, the first stage, to the final editing of the film. The second stage is the recording of any dialogue in the cartoon. After listening to the soundtrack of the dialogue, the director would then transfer that dialogue phonetically to an "exposure sheet," which indicates to the animators the mouth movements and facial expressions to be used on the characters.

# [ *chapter 3* ]

# THE TECHNIQUES OF INK AND PAINT

The first thing a painter has to learn is how to use the paint at the proper consistency. The paint needs to be stirred well and tested by lifting the paint stirrer to see how the paint drops back into the jar. Usually, the painter sitting next to you teaches you how to do this. Betty Hielborn was my teacher. Some painters liked working with thick paint, and some liked it very thin. There were others who liked it somewhere in between. Betty preferred the medium and, as a result, so did I. Those who liked the thin paint claimed they could work faster. As long as the paint looked opaque, the checker didn't mind. The main thing was to flow the paint on so that it didn't appear streaked when it dried.

Betty Brenon pointed out to me that every cel was numbered and that the paint had to be applied on the reverse side. The way to ensure that I was doing it correctly was to notice that the number would be on the left side and appear to be backwards. Betty also taught me that it was extremely important that I stay within the lines. But, she said, "If you should go over, use the wooden end of your paint brush to correct it." The ends of our brushes were sharpened in a pencil sharpener. However, we needed to be very careful in doing this, for if we scraped too hard, we could mar the cel.

Sometime later, someone discovered that solid ebony chopsticks, when sharpened, would not mar the cels. This practice became widespread throughout the industry. A group of us would go to Chinatown in downtown Los Angeles. Most of the stores down there carried those solid ebony chopsticks which, at that time, were only fifty cents a pair. Many of the other painters would give us orders and we would return with handsful. A few drinks and a delicious dinner made it a fun-filled evening. Our group, besides myself, consisted of Auril Thompson, Lee Hudson, Werdna Benning, Dea Shirley, and Dixie Mankameyer.

Someone once asked me if I made any mistakes. My answer was, "You name it. I did it." The first couple of months I was extra careful, and this made me considerably slower. At first, with every color I put on, I would turn the cel over to check it to ensure I didn't go over the line. If I did, I pushed the wet paint back with my scraper. I could do that if it wasn't too runny. By the time my scene was finished, it hardly needed any corrections done to it. But I still checked every cel again before I turned it in. People told me that that took too much time and that was what the checkers were paid for. However, I could never break this habit, even to my last day of work in the industry.

After three months, I was given my first raise, from $12.75 per week to $14.00! I guess I became complacent, and one day I painted a cel on the wrong side. As a result, the ink line came right off. My heart started pounding. I felt that I had committed a capital crime. But a wonderful inker named Leahadora DeSilva sat behind me. I told her what I had done. Her sympathetic response was, "Don't worry; wash it off cleanly and give it to me." I washed off the damaged parts on the face of the character, and she re-inked it in minutes. Boy, was I relieved! Sad to say, that was not the last time in my career that I painted the wrong side of the cel even though I promised myself it wouldn't happen again. It didn't make me feel any better that others did the same thing.

Another thing I'm sure I did plenty of times was to paint the wrong color. However, I can remember this happening only twice.

Could this be selective memory? The first time I used the wrong color, Betty Brenon angrily dumped a huge scene on my desk and pointed out my mistake. I had painted the wrong shade of brown on the wooden end of a rifle. I felt so stupid and ashamed. Ruthie Pierce showed me how to remove the incorrect color without taking off other painted parts of the cel it was touching.

She told me to take a tiny piece of toilet paper, put it on the part to be removed, and wet it with a brush dipped in clear water. She said that if I did six at a time, it would soften the paint so that it could be removed easily using the sharp end of the brush. What I learned that day came in handy for many years and enabled me to help others in the same situation.

The only other time I remember was when I painted the wrong shade of blue on Sniffles's hat. Sniffles was a little mouse created by Chuck Jones who appeared in twelve cartoons. This time, Betty again dumped the entire scene on my desk. Luckily, after I fixed it and brought it back to her, she was no longer angry. However, my feeling of stupidity lasted much longer.

One of the girls brought in an 8-ball from a pool set and, whenever someone made a glaring mistake, it was put on top of that girl's desk. It would remain there until someone else did something equally bad, or worse. This went on for several months. All of us took this like good sports until Gladys Hallberg, our checker, made a mistake—*big time*. She had let a scene get through that was painted wrong, and it came back from the camera department.

When the 8-ball was placed on her desk, she had a fit. The air was blue. She threw the ball away in the wastebasket, which ended our "behind the 8-ball game." It proved that anybody could make a mistake and it wouldn't be the end of the world.

Just by the nature of the job, inkers didn't make that many mistakes. I decided to practice inking at home. It took a while before I got the hang of it. Maxine Seaborn Cameron, who did beautiful inking, told me to use a very light touch and to look slightly ahead at the part of the line that was coming next.

When I thought that what I had done was good enough, I showed it to Frank Powers, the head of our ink and paint department. He said, "It looks o.k., but how long did it take you to do it?" I told him and he responded with, "No, you have to do it much faster." A few weeks later, I went to him again and told him that I was doing it faster. He gave me another excuse: "I don't need another inker at this time." Another time, he told me I was too good a painter and was needed in that position. I stopped asking him.

After we moved downstairs and Frank had left the studio, George Winkler became the new head of our department. When he found out I had been there over five years, he asked me how come I wasn't inking by now. I shrugged. He said, "There's no reason for you not to be inking. Try it." I did and became an inker on production in a day or two. I am grateful to him for that. At that time, an inker got five dollars a week more than a painter. But, the promotion, as little as it was, was good for my morale.

# [ *chapter 4* ]

# THE CAST OF CHARACTERS

When a character is first used in a cartoon, it is hard to tell if it will be just a one-time thing or if it will have that same magic that propelled Porky, Daffy, and "That Rabbit" to animated stardom.

It's been said many times that all of these stars had many "fathers." The directors, storymen, and animators created, wrote, and drew these characters so well that their personalities were infused with such realism that all of us and the viewing public thought about them as if they were actual living beings.

But can you picture what those animated cartoons would look like without the tender loving care of the members of the ink and paint department who traced those drawings exactly and painted those beautiful colors on the cels? That is what you see in the movie theatres or on television. Just like typical mothers, we worried and fretted about what those characters would look like out in public. So, you can see that we were concerned enough about them to do the best job possible. I must say that we enjoyed what we were doing and felt a great sense of pride and accomplishment when the picture was finished. What we didn't know back then was the lasting effect our "kids" would have on future generations.

# BOSKO

Bosko was the first Looney Tune star to appear on a movie screen in a Warner Bros. theatre or, for that matter, in movie houses across the United States. But he never set foot in a Warner Bros. cartoon studio. He actually did star in thirty-eight Looney Tunes. In many of them, he was joined by his girlfriend, Honey, and his dog, Bruno.

Hugh Harman created and registered Bosko for copyright in 1928, while Hugh was still working for Walt Disney. Both he and Rudy Ising worked for Disney in Kansas City. When Walt started his studio in California, he persuaded them to come out here to work for him. They worked on the "Alice in Cartoon Land" series plus "Oswald, the Lucky Rabbit."

After breaking away from Disney, Hugh and Rudy were hired by George Winkler and his sister Margaret, who was married to Charles Mintz. Universal Pictures was distributing their cartoons. However, after a year, Universal did not renew their contract; and Hugh, Rudy, and others, including Friz Freleng, Paul Smith, C. G. Maxwell, "Ham" Hamilton, Ben Clopton, and Ray Abrams found themselves out of a job.

Hugh and Rudy always yearned to produce their own cartoons. So, they and their newly unemployed buddies decided to make a test reel using the character that Hugh created and they named him "Bosko." They worked days and nights on this three-minute animated film. Sound had come in by then, and even though they were just animators, they figured out how to synchronize sound to the animation. This test reel was partly live action and partly animation, and they called it "Bosko, the Talk-ink Kid."

Rudy Ising was photographed at his drawing board and with his pen, he drew a little character who comes to life. Rudy talks to him and asks what he can do. Bosko tells him that he can sing and dance. After sampling his dancing technique, Rudy asks what else he can do. Bosko tells him that if he, Rudy, can draw a piano, he, Bosko, will play it while he sings. Rudy obliges. Bosko jumps on the piano stool

Bosko. A scene from "Big Hearted Bosko," released March 5, 1932, directed by Hugh Harman, animation by Isadore Freleng and Rollin Hamilton. Courtesy of Jerry Beck.

and starts to play and sing. A note comes loose from the piano. Bosko faces an imaginary audience and asks, "Ain't that a heck of a note?" He proceeds to play a very popular song of that day, "Sonny Boy." As he comes to the end of the song, he holds the last two notes, singing them so loudly that Rudy can't stand it any longer. He takes his fountain pen and sucks up all the lines he has drawn. He returns the ink to the ink bottle and puts the top on. We then see Bosko's head pop out, and he says, "So long, folks," and gives Rudy the raspberry. C. G. Maxwell did the voice of Bosko.

Rudy and Hugh shopped this film around to every known distributor they could find. After several months and many rejections, their luck changed. Stay tooned!

Leon Schlesinger started Pacific Title and Art in the mid-twenties. This company did all the main titles and dialogue cards for Warner Bros. With the advent of talking pictures, Leon realized that a big portion of his business would soon disappear. He was very friendly with Jack Warner and had helped finance *The Jazz Singer,* Warner Bros.'s first and very successful attempt at talking pictures. Warners also wanted to distribute cartoons to show in movie theatres, including their own. Jack Warner suggested to Leon that he get into the production of cartoons.

Even though Leon had no knowledge of how animation was done, he knew he would be able to handle such a venture, and he actually signed a contract with Warners before he had a company to do the work.

He didn't have to wait long, for, within a few days, someone arranged for him to meet with Hugh and Rudy and view their three-minute reel. Leon liked it and signed a three-year contract with them that very day. The studio became known as Harman-Ising Productions. I can't think of a more perfect name for a cartoon studio. The year was 1930.

All the Warner Bros. studio music was available to them. In fact, one of the provisions of their contract stipulated that they use songs and music from Warner Bros. feature films in all their cartoons.

Office space in a building at Western Avenue near Santa Monica Boulevard in Hollywood was rented. All the men who helped on the test reel went to work and, by May of that year, finished the first Bosko cartoon, "Sinkin' in the Bathtub." Four more Boskos followed that year. They were so successful that Jack Warner ordered another series that they named "Merrie Melodies." More people had to be hired and a larger studio had to be found. So, in 1931, Bosko and company moved to a building on Hollywood Boulevard near Wilton Place, from which they turned out seventeen cartoons that year.

In this year it was decided that the Looney Tunes would continue to be directed by Hugh Harman and that Rudy Ising would direct the new Merrie Melodies.

The first Merrie Melodie was "Lady, Play Your Mandolin" and came with a newly created character named Foxy. I use the newly created "Foxy" loosely for he looked just like Mickey Mouse, who had black round ears and a thin, long tail. Foxy had pointed ears and a bushy tail. Foxy's girlfriend, Piggy, looked just like Minnie Mouse except for the ears and tail.

Piggy is the lady with the madolin. I think that her name was a misnomer for Piggy was not a pig, but a fox.

Abe Lyman, who had a nationally known orchestra, provided the music for this cartoon and also for the next cartoon "Smile, Darn Ya, Smile."

The Merrie Melodies were just what you would expect, happy-go-lucky musical cartoons.

In 1933, when it came time to renew their contract, Hugh and Rudy wanted more money than Leon was willing to pay. These were depression years and Warner Bros. cut the amount of money they had agreed upon with Schlesinger. Leon refused to give Harman-Ising more. As a result, Harman-Ising split with Leon and took Bosko with them.

# BUDDY

When Leon Schlesinger organized his own studio without Hugh and Rudy, he needed a new character, and he wanted him as soon as possible. So, the first cartoon character to be born on the Warner Bros. old studio lot in Hollywood came into being quickly. Earl Duvall, one of the men hired away from Disney, came up with the character "Buddy," a little boy about the same size as Bosko, a do-gooder and rescuer like Bosko. Also like Bosko, Buddy had a girlfriend and a dog. His girlfriend's name was Cookie, and his dog's name was Towser. Jack Carr, an assistant animator, provided Buddy's voice.

Buddy had absolutely no charisma even though he was featured in twenty-three cartoons from 1933 to 1935. The Buddy pictures were the Looney Tunes. Fortunately, the Merrie Melodies made during that period were very entertaining and well accepted by the public.

## PORKY PIG

The first cartoon star that I became aware of at our studio was Porky Pig. At that time, he was quite obese, had a disgruntled expression on his face, and stuttered so badly he could hardly be understood. I found that the reason for this was that the actor, Joe Dougherty, actually did stutter, but was not able to control it. During recording sessions, he became very frustrated and the directors and sound editor almost went crazy.

Model sheet of Porky Pig to show size and how Porky should be drawn. © Warner Bros. Entertainment, Inc. Martha Goldman Sigall Collection.

They worked with him for almost two years until the fabulous voice actor Mel Blanc came along and took over Porky's voice. Mel was not only able to master the stuttering perfectly but, in doing so, gave Porky a more likeable personality at the same time.

The animators started to draw him a lot cuter. His body lines and facial features became more defined, and he was much easier for us to ink and paint.

Leon Schlesinger loved Porky Pig. I had heard that he didn't care that much for Bosko and didn't like Buddy at all. I really believe he

Lobby card for "Calling Dr. Porky," released September 21, 1940, directed by I. Freleng, animation by Herman Cohen, musical direction by Carl W. Stalling. Porky Pig, M.D., treats an intoxicated patient who sees pink elephants. © Warner Bros. Entertainment, Inc. Courtesy of Jerry Beck.

considered Porky Pig his "first born." When he went into the story room to pass out checks on payday, he would always look at the storyboards. If he didn't see Porky up there, he'd ask, "How come Porky isn't in this cartoon?" The guys would tell him, "Porky will be in the next one." They would make special drawings of Porky and tack them up in strategic places throughout the storyboard. When "Papa" came in the following week, he'd see those drawings of Porky and smile and remark, "This looks like it will be a very funny cartoon."

Porky was usually unsophisticated and good natured until someone was out to get him. Then he'd get angry and fight back, but he didn't always win—sort of like real life. He had the same "M.O." in later years, too. Poor Porky.

## DAFFY DUCK

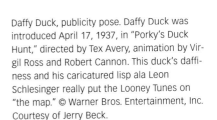

"DAFFY DUCK"

Tex Avery, one of our cartoon directors, used Porky several times in his early cartoons. One of these was called "Porky's Duck Hunt." Of course, knowing Tex, his duck would not be your run-of-the-mill kind of duck. His duck was so zany and completely daffy, he drove poor Porky out of his mind. In the opening scene, Daffy is a "sitting duck" in a lake, but he did not stay that way long. He started woo-wooing all over the place with his crazy antics, skimming all over the lake, leaving Porky completely bewildered. It was a very funny cartoon, and Daffy Duck became an instant star when his first cartoon was released April 17, 1937.

Daffy Duck, publicity pose. Daffy Duck was introduced April 17, 1937, in "Porky's Duck Hunt," directed by Tex Avery, animation by Virgil Ross and Robert Cannon. This duck's daffiness and his caricatured lisp ala Leon Schlesinger really put the Looney Tunes on "the map." © Warner Bros. Entertainment, Inc. Courtesy of Jerry Beck.

In Daffy's subsequent pictures, he doesn't "woo-woo" as often, but he does play tricks on other characters. He becomes such an egotistical, selfish, and scheming individual that everyone is happy when he gets his comeuppance at the end.

Daffy was in hundreds of cartoons and lasted until Warner Bros. closed its cartoon unit. There was no fiftieth birthday celebration for him like the year-long celebration for Bugs Bunny when he turned fifty, and Daffy didn't get a star on the Hollywood Walk of Fame as did Bugs. So far as I know, the only honor he has received was the issuance of a United States postage stamp in the year 2000. They sold very well at the Post Office, from what I've heard.

## BUGS BUNNY

Daffy Duck came into being before Bugs Bunny. This is the story of how Bugs Bunny was "born" and how he got his name. In the early 1930s, there was a storyman at Schlesinger's who also directed a few pictures during his stay there; his name was Ben Hardaway. One day, he told me he was "going to put a rabbit suit on that duck," meaning that he was going to create a character that would look like a rabbit but have the crazy personality of Daffy Duck.

The cartoon he envisioned using this character was "Porky's Hare Hunt," co-directed by himself and Cal Dalton. The rabbit was white, and it did act very much like Daffy Duck. The only thing this rabbit did like the present-day Bugs Bunny was his utterance of the words, "Of course, you know this means war!"

When the cartoon was released, the public liked it very much. The studio received phone calls and letters and even heard that people were stopping by the box office of the theatres wanting to know when they would see more of "that rabbit."

The studio decided to make another rabbit picture, and Chuck Jones was assigned to do it. He and his unit, using the same white rabbit, did a cartoon called "Prest-O Change-O." It was about two dogs fleeing a dog catcher. They wander into a magician's house and encounter a white rabbit. There is no dialogue throughout the cartoon. The action revolves around the dogs and the rabbit engaged in one magic trick after another.

When it was screened at the studio, we all really liked it. There were a lot of laughs and much applause. I also saw it in a theatre, and the audience thought it was hilarious. The first rabbit picture, "Porky's Hare Hunt," had produced many requests for more, and so did this one. The public actually asked for them.

The two dogs were used in two other cartoons, but no one asked about them. However, there were more letters and cards about "that rabbit." The studio brass thought, "Maybe, we're on to something" and decided to make another rabbit cartoon. They assigned Ben Hardaway and Cal Dalton again. The name of this next cartoon was "Hare-Um-Scare-Um" and, it was decided that this time the rabbit would be gray instead of white.

The directors had Charlie Thorson, a character designer, draw a model sheet of this rabbit. A model sheet is drawn to show the character from all the different angles he would appear in the cartoon, from the front, from the back, from the left, from the right. This was to enable the animators, assistants, and inbetweeners, to draw the character uniformly throughout the cartoon, for no matter how many of them worked on the picture, (there could be three or four, there could be fifteen or twenty), the characters had to look the same throughout.

When Charlie finished his model sheet, he labeled it "Bugs' Bunny." And why did he do that? Because "Bugs" was Ben Hardaway's nickname.

"Hare-Um-Scare-Um" was a big hit with the public. So another rabbit picture was assigned, this time to Chuck Jones, who directed a picture entitled "Elmer's Candid Camera." This rabbit was also gray and had some of the physical features of the rabbit from "Hare-Um-Scare-Um." And, once again, this picture was very well received by the public.

In production at the same time as "Elmer's Candid Camera" was "A Wild Hare," directed by Tex Avery. He, too, made a few changes on the rabbit. He asked a young layout artist named Bob Givens to make a new model sheet. Tex is the one who gave the rabbit the expression, "What's up, Doc." And, it was in this cartoon that the rabbit's voice was changed to that of "a tough little Brooklyn or Bronx stinker," as Mel Blanc described it.

It wasn't until 1940, after this picture was released, that this "star" needed a name. Rose Horsely, our publicist, the storymen, and the directors got together to think up the perfect name for that rabbit. Tex suggested "Jack E. Rabbit." That got a thumbs down. Several

Motion picture trade ad touting Bugs Bunny as a new cartoon star from Leon Schlesinger Productions. © Warner Bros. Entertainment, Inc. Courtesy of Jerry Beck.

other names were bantered about, but discarded. Then Rose looked at a board containing a number of model sheets and noticed the one that said "Bugs' Bunny," and she exclaimed, "What about Bugs Bunny?" Tex's response was "Nah, that's a fuzzy-wuzzy name." Everyone else just shrugged. Rose said, "I'm going to ask the old man." Going into Leon's office, she asked, "How do you like the name Bugs Bunny for our rabbit?" Immediately, he said, "I like it." And, that's how Bugs Bunny got his name.

Word of the naming of that rabbit got around the studio quickly. We all heard about it that very same day.

The next rabbit picture was "Elmer's Pet Rabbit." For the first time, the title read, "Featuring Bugs Bunny." A few other cartoons that followed read the same way. But, soon after, the title was changed to "Starring Bugs Bunny."

Fairly soon after the Warner Bros. Museum opened in 1996, there was a special opening for the people who then worked in the animation department. At this time, the whole second floor of the museum was devoted to animation. At the back of the room, there were two thick plastic panels with about two feet of space between them. Behind and to the left side of the back panel, there was a backdrop of the piano from the cartoon "Carrotblanca," a takeoff of the feature film *Casablanca*. The actual piano was on display on the first floor of the museum.

The back panel, on the left side, had a large drawing of Bugs Bunny on it. The right side of the front panel had a drawing of Daffy Duck. People could go between the two panels, make faces at Bugs or Daffy, sit on a small bench and pretend to play the piano, and so on. A camera and monitor were rigged up in front of these panels, and we were able to take pictures of people posing with the characters. There was also a processing machine that could print the picture in just over a minute. This enabled us to give the visitors a picture of themselves with Bugs and Daffy to take home.

The line waiting to have their pictures taken the night of the animation employees' party extended from the back of the room to the front. On this particular evening, there must have been two hundred people waiting in line. My husband, Sol, who is also a docent, had an interesting time with these people from Warner Bros. Animation. He thought to himself, "How can I keep all these people occupied and entertained while waiting to have their picture taken?" Knowing all the answers in advance, he approached the first group of about ten and asked, "You people are from Warner Bros. Animation, aren't you?" They answered, "Yes." He then said, "I want to give you Warner Bros. trivia question number one. Can any of you tell me the name of the character on the back panel?" Everyone looked at the panel and then looked at him as though he were from Mars or some other far-off place. "Everyone in the world knows Bugs Bunny and he's asking us who that character is?" For a short while that seemed like a long while, no one answered. Finally, one girl said, "Do you mean Bugs Bunny?" He replied, "Yes, that's right. Now for Warner Bros. trivia question number two. Can any one of you tell me how Bugs Bunny got his name?"

Would you believe it? Of all the people there that evening from Warner Bros. Animation, not one person was able to tell him the story you have just read! I guess this is not really as strange as it seems. The visitors were of an entirely different generation from the 1930s and either didn't think to ask or had no one to ask who could give them the answer. They may not even have known there was a story about the naming of Bugs. Working as docents at the museum since it opened, Sol and I have had many occasions to tell this story over and over again to the museum visitors.

## ELMER FUDD, NEE EGGHEAD

There is something that can happen only in an animated cartoon— one character is able to evolve and become another! Such is the case of Egghead, who was created by Tex Avery and first appeared in "Egghead Rides Again," released in 1937. As far as his physical

Elmer Fudd became the most famous "wabbit" hunter of all time. © Warner Bros. Entertainment, Inc. Courtesy of Jerry Beck.

Lobby card for "Egghead Rides Again." Released July 17, 1937. Created and directed by Tex Avery; animation by Paul Smith and Irvin Spence; musical direction by Carl W. Stalling. The first Egghead cartoon with the persona and voice type of then-current comedian Joe Penner. After almost a dozen cartoons, Egghead evolved into Elmer Fudd. © Warner Bros. Entertainment, Inc. Courtesy of Jerry Beck.

appearance goes, the name Egghead suited him perfectly. His head and all his facial features were oval shaped, like an egg. Although an "egghead" is a person who is highly intellectual, Egghead was the complete opposite, a real buffoon, in all his nine pictures.

The voice they gave him suited him. It was very nasal, like the old radio comic Joe Penner. I'm sure it was Tex who picked that type of voice to suit Egghead's personality.

In an Egghead picture entitled "A Feud There Was," he plays the part of a peacemaker between feuding hillbilly families. He rides a little motorcycle with a sign on the side carrying the name of Elmer J. Fudd. Aha! That portents of things to come. Tex could have done this purposely. He always knew what he was doing.

A few cartoons later, in March 1940, in a Chuck Jones picture, a character comes along who, likewise, is dumb, if not dumber, than Egghead. This character has a perfectly round head. His facial appearance is different, but he wears the same outfit worn by Egghead in quite a few of his pictures, clothing such as a brown derby, a white wing collar, a gold cravat, a green coat, and green pants. It was in this cartoon that an early Bugs Bunny, although he doesn't have this name as yet, antagonizes this unfortunate character. The name of this cartoon is "Elmer's Candid Camera." We understood immediately—Egghead was now Elmer Fudd. Arthur Q. Bryan, of radio and television's Fibber McGee and Molly fame, did the voice.

Another cartoon with Elmer released the same month was "Confederate Honey," directed by Friz Freleng.

Then, in July, "A Wild Hare," directed by Tex Avery, shows Elmer, for the first time, as a hunter, and we hear him saying, "Be vewy, vewy quiet. I'm hunting wabbits." And, for the first time, we hear Bugs ask, "What's up, Doc?" This is the cartoon that made Bugs a star and established Elmer as his foil for many, many years.

## SNIFFLES, NEE TOMMY CAT

Something that is also possible to change in a cartoon is the species of an animal. A little character by the name of Tommy Cat had his first and last appearance in the very first cartoon that Chuck Jones directed, "The Night Watchman." Several months later, the character with approximately the same look became a mouse named Sniffles.

Sniffles was a lot of fun to ink and paint because he was so cute, but this character lasted for just twelve cartoons. We all liked him because he was so sweet and not rough or tough.

Model sheet of Sniffles showing him from every angle. Chuck Jones introduced him in "Naughty but Mice." © Warner Bros. Entertainment, Inc. Courtesy of Jerry Beck.

## INKI

Inki was a darling little boy from the jungle of Africa. There were three pictures made featuring him: "Little Lion Hunter," "Inki and the Lion," and "Inki and the Minah Bird." All three of these cartoons were very clever and funny and were all directed by Chuck Jones. I don't know why he didn't become a continuing character. Two more Inki cartoons were made in later years. None of them are shown on television because they all are considered politically incorrect.

## CONRAD CAT

Conrad Cat appeared in only three cartoons: "Porky's Café," in black and white; "Conrad the Sailor" and "The Bird Came C.O.D.," both in color. Those of us in the ink and paint department always thought Conrad looked like a caricature of Chuck Jones, who had directed all three of these cartoons.

## TWEETY

While I was with Leon Schlesinger, I got to work on the very first Tweety picture, "A Tale of Two Kitties." In it, Tweety was a baby bird and his body was painted a flesh color. But, he grew up fast, thanks to the Hays Office, an organization that was formed by the movie producers to see that the content of feature films and animated cartoons remained "squeaky clean." They insisted that the bird have yellow feathers instead of being "naked," for they felt it would not be proper for children to view him in this way.

I remember he had the name "Orson" before the more suitable name of Tweety was given to him. He always spoke like a baby bird, voiced by Mel Blanc, and, even in his first picture, he uttered the famous statement, "I tawt I taw a puddy tat."

Bob Clampett created Tweety and directed his first two films. After I left Schlesinger's in 1943 and Bob left in 1946, Friz Freleng redesigned Tweety with a larger head and smaller feet and teamed him with a character he created named Sylvester. What could be a better combination than a cat and a canary? Their first picture together was "Tweety Pie" and it was an instant success, winning the Oscar for 1947. This team won their second Oscar in 1957 for "Birds Anonymous." All in all, Friz made forty cartoons starring this duo.

The characters that I've mentioned were all created during my seven-year tenure with Leon Schlesinger. Warner Bros. Cartoons created and developed many more personalities such as Sylvester, Pepe

This model sheet of Tweety was designed for the Friz Freleng unit. The cartoon "Tweetie Pie" won the Academy Award for 1947. © Warner Bros. Entertainment, Inc. Warner Bros. Corporate Archives.

LePew, Speedy Gonzales, Foghorn Leghorn, Hippety Hopper, the Road Runner, Wile E. Coyote, Yosemite Sam, the Tasmanian Devil, Marvin Martian, Goofy Gophers, and others.

In later years, while working for several different ink and paint services, Celine Miles, C&D Ink and Paint, and Mary Cain, I did get to work on many of the newer characters. Working on those Warner Bros. characters, I felt I had come full circle.

The name "Acme" appears in so many of the Warner Bros. cartoons that I felt it should be properly included in this list of "characters."

# ACME

As far as I know, an "Acme" product was first used in "Buddy's Bug Hunt," a cartoon that was released in 1935. Actually, it was used twice in this picture, first as a box of some sort of powder. It was impossible to tell what the box contained for the cartoon characters, spiders, blocked the lettering describing the product. This powder was poured on Buddy while he was encased in a spider web. Secondly, the wording is very visible at the top of "Acme Fly Paper." Letters of the alphabet were thrown at it and stuck to it forming words condemning Buddy for cruelty to bugs.

At this point in time, I would guess that only members of the studio staff would have taken notice of this use of the Acme name.

In another cartoon in 1938, "Porky's Poppa," Poppa makes a telephone call and asks, "Hello, Acme Company?" There were a few snickers in our screening room, but I will bet it went unnoticed by theatre audiences. Of course, present-day cartoon buffs notice everything!

To my knowledge, our studio and others bought calibrated pegboards, sliding cel boards, inking boards and, perhaps, other pieces of equipment from a company called Acme Camera Corporation located in Burbank, California. I heard the name "Acme" used in the studio from time to time, so it wasn't any surprise to me that storymen threw that name into a cartoon. They had a habit of using inside gags all the time. They even went to the extent of using caricatures of the guys at the studio, Henry Binder, Cal Dalton, Ken Harris, and others, but nothing else caught on like Acme.

# [ *chapter 5* ]

# PRODUCTION
# TERMINOLOGY

You may have noticed that I used the term "sliding cel boards." Rod Scribner, an animator, referred to these as "biff-sniffs." This name stuck and became popular throughout the industry. No matter what studio one worked for, these boards were always called biff-sniffs—perhaps even to this day.

For the first few months that I was an apprentice painter, I concentrated completely on my job, learning how to apply the paint and how to follow the action correctly. I hardly noticed what anyone else was doing.

Being seated between two experienced painters, Sylvia Rogers and Betty Hielborn, made it easier for me. If I had any questions, I would ask Betty, who was very helpful. When she suddenly quit the studio, I felt lost. Almost immediately, though, Betty Brenon told me I was going to be moved into the middle of the room, with a desk on the aisle. She and Art Goble had their desks across the aisle and against the wall. Perhaps they moved me near them in order to better keep an eye on what I was doing. The other women in my row were inkers. Seated next to me was Frances Ewing.

I soon noticed that the inkers traced their drawings on a 12" x 14" metal board that was equipped with two round pegs at the top and bottom of the board. The three-peg system wasn't used until the 1950s, about the same time acetate cels came into use. Since the papers with the drawings were punched with two holes, the cels, of course, had to be punched the same. In that way, the inked cel would have the animation in the correct position.

Most of the cels would be short twelve-field cels, but some scenes required longer cels, which we referred to as "two-field" or "three-field" cels. The drawings would be stamped with instructions to the inkers as to what size cels were to be used. Long cels were used when the background moved with the animation. If the character, for example, was running, the cameraman would accomplish this by moving the background while, at the same time, moving the cel showing the character in the next running position. This would be repeated throughout the scene.

Some drawings were stamped REG. to B.G. (Register to Background). That meant part of the character was touching something on the background. For, example, if Porky Pig is seated on a chair that is part of the background, the part of him that touches the chair must match or "register" exactly to the chair. There cannot be any space showing. To accomplish this, the inker puts the background on her ink board and inks each cel, carefully matching his sitting parts to the outline of the chair.

Sitting next to Frances was like getting an education in inking techniques. One day, I heard her tell Art that she needed to use the biff-sniff. Art said, "O.K." and left the room to get it. Noticing my double-take, Frances told me a biff-sniff was a nickname for a sliding cel board. "And why do you need a sliding cel board, and what is a sliding cel board?" I asked. She told me that it is a large, round, flat disk with ruled metal strips top and bottom. Each strip had four sets of pegs and moved on a track. Still not understanding fully, I watched as she used it.

The cartoon being inked was a Friz Freleng Merrie Melodie called "Coo Coo Nut Grove." The main characters were caricatures of

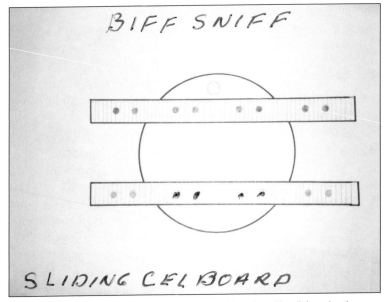

Biff-sniff. Rod Scribner dubbed this name for a sliding cel board used by all the animation departments when the animation and background move at the same time. Martha Goldman Sigall Collection.

movie stars and well-known entertainers attending a nightclub. This was a spoof of the famous Los Angeles nightclub, the Cocoanut Grove.

The scene Frances was working on caricatured Helen Morgan, whose trademark was sitting on top of a baby grand piano while she sang her torch songs. Frances had inked everything except the part of Helen's body that touched the piano on the background. To continue, she placed the long background on the top pegs of the biff-sniff. Then she placed a long cel of Helen Morgan on the bottom pegs. She moved both tracks according to the instructions to the point where Helen's body, on the lower track, met the piano on the upper track. This enabled her to complete the inking. She had more than a hundred of these cels and it was very time consuming.

Being so fascinated by what I had just seen, I asked Betty Brenon if I could work on that scene when the picture came to the painters.

She had to divide the scene up among us, but she did give me a portion of it. Of course, there was nothing special that we painters had to do but paint it in the usual manner and handle the long cels carefully.

I remember this incident well because I had learned a new technique in the making of animated cartoons. This cartoon, in particular, fascinated me for it was my first experience painting movie stars. "Coo Coo Nut Grove" was an outstanding picture. The last scene was the one of Helen Morgan. She begins singing "The Little Things You Used to Do" and, as the song goes on, she starts to cry. All the movie stars start crying, too, even tough guys like George Raft and Edward G. Robinson. The tears flood the nightclub to the point that the piano floats completely out of the picture as the cartoon ends.

When cartoons were screened for us during my first few months in the studio, I would look only for what I had done in each of them. But when "Coo Coo Nut Grove" came on the screen, I looked beyond what I had done, noticing for the first time all the technical aspects, the camera angles, the great animation, and the beautiful backgrounds. It was at this point that I acquired a real appreciation for the way cartoons were made. Tee Hee (Thornton Hee), one of our animators, had designed the caricatures for this picture.

Subsequently, I learned many more techniques sitting next to Frances. She was a very industrious inker, not at all the type to chitchat about personal or inconsequential happenings.

When Art Goble left to head the ink and paint department at MGM, we were all devastated. He took several inkers with him, and he wanted Frances to be one of them, but she refused. I didn't know it at that time, but she was planning to marry that wonderful animator and, more important, that wonderful guy, Virgil Ross. It wasn't until we all received an invitation to her bridal shower given by Myrn Stevenson, Margurite Connor, and Celine Miles that I, her seatmate, found out about the coming nuptials.

# [ *chapter 6* ]

# THE BOYS OF
# TERMITE TERRACE

During the time I worked in animation, I met and worked with many of the well-known people in our field. The following are but a few of these people. My comments are strictly personal and result from my own contact with each of them.

## FRED ("TEX") AVERY

Tex Avery began his illustrious career as an inker, as so many other cartoon directors did. He was working for Walter Lantz on the Oswald series during 1928. He soon became an inbetweener and contributed gags for the pictures. By 1930, he was animating. Bill Nolan, Lantz's partner, realized Tex's ability and let him do a storyboard. After looking it over, Bill told him to lay it out and hand out the work to the animators. Essentially, he was directing pictures without getting any such credit.

Tex was dating a pretty inker named Pat and they were planning to get married. Since he did so much around the studio, he asked for a fifteen dollars a week raise, but was turned down by the Universal executives. So he quit.

He and Pat got married, had a wonderful honeymoon in Oregon, and came back broke. Tex decided to go to Leon Schlesinger's, telling Leon he was a director. Leon took him at his word. The timing was perfect for Leon was very unhappy with the character Buddy and with one of his directors. Leon wanted to use animal characters a la Disney. Tex convinced Leon to let him try to improve his animated cartoons. Leon said, "O.K., I'll take a chance on you and let you do one cartoon. I'll give you some young, talented animators who aren't happy in their respective units."

This new unit would be made up of Chuck Jones, Robert ("Bobo") Cannon, and Bob Clampett. Tex agreed and recommended two former buddies from Lantz, Virgil Ross and Sid Sutherland. Leon hired them. Yes, Leon was a gambling man and, with this crew, I'd say he hit the jackpot. These men would bring recognition to the future of animation. They were all filled with enthusiasm and ambition and worked day and night. They were placed in the middle of the old Warner Bros. lot in a ramshackled building that they immediately dubbed "Termite Terrace." The rest of Leon's employees remained in the building at the north end of the studio, near Sunset Boulevard.

The first cartoon this unit produced was "Gold Diggers of '49" with Porky and Beans. Evidently, Leon was pleased with their efforts, for this was followed by "The Blow Out" and "Plane Dippy." Only the storyboard, layout, and animation were done by this unit. The backgrounds, ink and paint, music, camera, and editing were done at the Sunset Boulevard location.

Leon thought it would be better if all the staff worked in the same building because Termite Terrace really was falling apart. He procured and slightly renovated a two-story building on the southeast side of the lot, at Van Ness Avenue and Fernwood. How lucky for me that Leon made this move, for that is where I came upon him while he was watching men paint his name on the side of the building.

Tex was one of the few directors who would come up to the ink and paint department. I think he liked seeing how his cartoons were turning out. He would answer questions and was always in a good humor. There was always a lot of wild action taking place in his cartoons. Some of the girls would complain, kiddingly of course. He would always explain his ideas and the reason it had to be done that way.

One picture that I remember was called "Screwball Football." The first half was rather ordinary technically, and then the announcer character would say, "It's half-time and we'll now change sides." Of course, if you knew Tex, you'd know that the teams would not be changing sides. Instead, the spectators changed sides! As they moved from one side to the other, they had to intermingle and we had to follow through with the correct colors. What a job! We almost went blind and were close to going crazy. Tex was in our department daily during that part. He tried assuring us that it would all work out right. When it was screened, it went so fast, we wondered why we had fretted so much about it. As shown on television these days, that scene looks doctored and not the way I remembered it.

A cartoon of his that really impressed me was released in 1937 and titled "I Only Have Ice for You." All of the characters were cartoon-type birds. The hero (voiced by Joe Twerp, a radio comedian who spoke in spoonerisms), who drives an ice truck, does his best to avoid the amorous advances of a homely bird who is trying her hardest to win him with her baking and cooking. He, however, wants to win the affections of a very pretty bird who tells him that the only kind of bird she could be interested in would have to be a great crooner.

Not being able to sing, our hero hires a music professor who is also a ventriloquist. The student arranges for Professor Mocking Bird to sit in the back of the student's ice truck and sing as he drives and lip-syncs. His female interest snuggles up to him. However, as the song goes on, Professor Mocking Bird gets colder and colder and begins to shudder and shake so hard that the back of his truck comes open, exposing our hero in his act. In the end, it is the professor who wins the girl. Our hero succumbs to the homely bird and her cooking.

This cartoon was reissued with the Blue Ribbon title of "I Only Have Eyes for You." Many of the old-time cartoons, when reissued, had a blue ribbon added to the title page and all the credits removed. I was very surprised to see the original title changed and inquired of many of the people with whom I worked at Leon Schlesinger. "Do you remember the cartoon 'I Only Have Eyes for You'" The response I always got was, "You mean 'I Only Have Ice for You.'" From Mark Kausler, I learned that the title was copyrighted in 1937 under the name "I Only Have Eyes for You?" Perhaps the cartoon that was screened for us was just a working title of "I Only Have Ice for You." This pun is used in the musical portion of the cartoon.

Here are some of the people I put this question to: Bob Matz, Tom Ray, Virgil Ross, Chuck Jones, and Norm McCabe. To my knowledge, it is the only Schlesinger or Warner Bros. cartoon title that had ever been changed. That is a bit of trivia unknown to many people.

Tex left Leon Schlesinger in 1941. There are several versions of how and why he left. The one that I remember is a disagreement with Leon over the ending of a cartoon Tex directed called "The Heckling Hare." Bugs Bunny is cavorting with a dog all through the picture and both of them fall off a cliff, but they land on their feet and Bugs says, looking at the audience, "We fooled ya, didn't we?" They manage to get to the top and fall off again. Bugs says, "Here we go again," and they land on their feet again. During each fall, there is lots of yelling and screaming. Leon objected to the repetitious second fall and told Tex to cut it from the cartoon. Being a perfectionist and wanting to be in control of his picture, Tex insisted that it remain in. However, Leon, as the boss, won the dispute and got his way. Tex was suspended and never came back to the studio.

For a short time, Tex worked at Jerry Fairbanks's studio on a series that he, Tex, created called "Speaking of Animals." This series involved live-action animals with animated mouths and eyes. Tex did only three of these pictures and then sold the series to Jerry Fairbanks, who produced them for another seven years.

Tex was offered and accepted a job at MGM and directed some of the funniest cartoons until he left there in 1956. I worked there from 1946 to 1950 and, as always, it was great working with Tex. I once asked him, "Do you miss the Looney Tune characters?" His response was, "Sometimes, but I don't miss anything else. MGM is a heck of a better place to work, in every way, and the people here are just as great."

# BOB CLAMPETT

Bob Clampett was an enthusiastic and fun type of a guy who was always nice to me and very generous when I was collecting for some cause, gifts, or chances on a raffle.

When I started back in 1936, Bob was an animator. He started with the Harman-Ising Studio in 1931 as an inbetweener. His first animation credit came in January of 1934 on a Merrie Melodie, "Pettin' in the Park." He probably animated sooner than 1934, but the studio was strange the way it rotated screen credits. There were always at least four animators in each director's unit. But, sometimes, only one and rarely two, received screen credit. Bob's next screen credit didn't come until October of that year, in a cartoon entitled "Shake Your Powder Puff," directed by Friz Freleng.

I had heard that Leon Schlesinger was very anxious to have a new cartoon star. He lost Bosko when Rudy Ising and Hugh Harman left, taking their character with them. As I have mentioned, Buddy was the brainchild of Earl Duvall. Although he was in quite a few pictures, he was never an endearing or interesting character. There was also a minor character called Goopy Geer who didn't catch on either. According to the story, Leon offered a monetary prize to the guys if they could come up with a new and interesting character. He even suggested using a format based on the Our Gang comedies.

The guys decided to take his suggestion and do a cartoon called "I Haven't Got a Hat," which was going to be directed by Friz Freleng and take place in a schoolroom setting. So, a few of them got together to create some little characters.

Rollin ("Ham") Hamilton was one of the animators on the cartoon, and someone suggested using two puppies and calling them "Ham and Ex." Bob Clampett thought that if "Ham and Ex" were good enough, what about "Porky and Beans?" Porky would be a fat, stuttering pig and Beans a mischievous cat. Then, someone suggested "Oliver Owl," who was to be a snooty kind of character, a real know-it-all. The teacher of the gang would be a cow named "Miss Cud."

All the kids would perform various little acts for their parents. Porky recited and acted out "The Midnight Ride of Paul Revere." The two little puppies sang "I Haven't Got a Hat," and the little kitty recited "Mary Had a Little Lamb." Oliver Owl played the piano. This is the first picture in which Porky Pig appeared.

Porky and Beans appeared in Tex Avery's first cartoon, "Gold Diggers of '49," for which Bob Clampett and Chuck Jones received animation credit.

Porky and Beans were together in another cartoon entitled "Boom Boom." Then, Beans starred in "Alpine Antics" with Porky in a nonspeaking role. Beans was featured in "A Cartoonist's Nightmare," "Hollywood Capers," and "The Phantom Ship." This was the end of Beans. Ham and Ex starred in one more cartoon called "The Fire Alarm," but their demise came soon after in "Westward Whoa." Porky, however, survived to become Leon Schlesinger's first star.

Leon Schlesinger decided that he would have Ub Iwerks direct three cartoons at his own studio in Beverly Hills. Although Ub had a full staff, Leon wanted Bob and Chuck to go there to do the animation so that it would be in the style of our studio. Florence Finkelhor, an inker in our studio at the time, was sent along with them to head the ink and paint department. Leon wanted the style of inking to be the same, too.

The cartoons they turned out were "Porky and Gabby," "Porky's Super Service," and "Porky's Badtime Story." After the first two, from what I have heard, Ub lost interest and Leon picked Bob to supervise the third cartoon. A new unit was assigned to him, and they were located in the Sunset Boulevard building, which had been renovated and was occupied by the Ray Katz unit, with Ray being named the producer.

Two of these cartoons had featured Porky and Gabby Goat, a very unlikeable character, which didn't help make the cartoons successful.

Even though "Porky's Badtime Story" was not a smash hit, it solidified Bob Clampett's position as a director. He went on to direct many Porky Pig and other cartoons. One of my favorites was "Porky in Wackyland" released in 1938. This picture has since become a classic.

Everyone in the Sunset Boulevard building remained there for another couple of years until recalled in 1941 to the location on Van Ness Avenue, which had been remodeled. Our ink and paint department was merged with the girls from the Katz unit, and we were all put in one big room on the first floor. Instead of there being forty women, there were now sixty of us.

Bob and his unit continued to do Looney Tunes in black and white, with Porky Pig. In 1941, though, Bob directed his first Merrie Melodie in color, "Goofy Groceries." This picture was well received by all the studio people.

Another Merrie Melodie, "Farm Frolics," soon followed, and Bob's first Bugs Bunny cartoon, "Wacky Wabbit," was released in 1942.

When Tex Avery left in 1941, Bob took over Tex's unit and completed the unfinished cartoons "Cagey Canary" and "Crazy Cruise." Next, he directed one of my favorite cartoons, "Horton Hatches the Egg," from a story by Dr. Seuss. Dr. Seuss was the nom de plume of Ted Geisel. Ted worked at the studio while the story was being written. Mike Maltese, from our story department, worked on the gags. It was a great cartoon and narrated completely in rhyme.

Horton, a pink elephant, agrees to sit on a nest for Mayzie, a very irresponsible bird who has laid an egg but leaves on vacation. She promises to come back soon. However, she is gone for a long, long time but, Horton, true to his word, sits on the nest saying over and over again, "I meant what I said and I said what I meant, an elephant's faithful 100 percent." He laments this phrase many times through rain, sleet, and snow. Many months go by. Horton is still sitting on the nest. Finally, hunters accost Horton, who won't budge. So they remove him by force, still sitting on the nest, and sell him to a circus.

While Horton is appearing in a sideshow, Mayzie suddenly drops in, demanding her egg back. At that point, the egg hatches, and out comes a flying baby elephant. Horton and "his son" go back to the jungle singing the "Hut-Sut" song. This is a beautiful and colorful cartoon. It was a big hit with the public.

Bob went on to direct many more great cartoons. He created Tweety, who has become a world famous cartoon character.

Bob directed a cartoon that can only be described as a masterpiece, "Coal Black and de Sebben Dwarfs," released in 1943. The main char-

"Horton Hatches an Egg." Released April 11, 1942. Directed by Bob Clampett, animation by Bob McKimson, story by Dr. Seuss (aka Ted Geisel), gags by Mike Maltese, musical direction by Carl W. Stalling. Pictured is Mayzie charming Horton the elephant to sit on an egg she just laid while she goes on vacation. © Warner Bros. Entertainment, Inc. Courtesy of Jerry Beck.

acters were designed by Gene Hazelton, who also drew the model sheets. The storyman was Warren Foster. Rod Scribner was the only animator to receive screen credit. But, since each directorial unit consisted of four animators, three others must have animated on it as well plus their assistants and the inbetweeners.

The layouts, backgrounds, animation, and camera angles were superb. Its fast-moving pace was dizzyingly clever. The jazzy music and sound were raucous but quite appropriate to fit the action. In my opinion at that time, from a technical point of view, this was one of the best cartoons ever produced. When the picture was screened for the studio employees, they were moved to screaming and thunderous applause. But, regrettably, it is considered politically incorrect today and its artistic, technical, and historic interest is not widely known.

Bob also directed "Snafu" training films during World War II, as well as "Any Bonds Today?" starring Bugs Bunny selling war bonds. As with most other cartoons, this film was shown in theatres all across the country. Between feature films (these were the days of double features on most programs) or between these features and the cartoon, the theatre lights would come on and ushers would pass jars around for the audience to drop in monetary contributions to help finance the war effort. It was hoped that this film would motivate the public to buy savings bonds.

Some of the other classic cartoons directed by Bob Clampett were "Tortoise Wins by a Hare," "A Corny Concerto," "Falling Hare," and "What's Cookin', Doc?"

I left the studio in 1943 and didn't see Bob again until 1960, when he produced the animated series of "Beany and Cecil" at his new studio, Snowball. At the time, I was doing freelance painting and was picking up work to do at home. It was good to renew old acquaintances with Raynelle Day, a friend from Leon Schlesinger's, who was Bob's ink and paint supervisor, and others I had worked with at different studios.

Bob left Warner Bros. in 1946 to produce commercials and "Beany and Cecil," which started out as a puppet show and became a nationwide hit.

A number of years later, Bob had an RCA–Columbia Pictures contract to produce a series of home videos of his "Beany and Cecil" cartoons. He toured the country promoting this venture. I was saddened to learn that on May 4, 1984, while in Detroit, Michigan, he suffered a heart attack and died. He was only seventy.

Bob always had so much enthusiasm for the cartoon business, and I still hear from people of how he helped them in their wish to get into the animation business and went on to mentor them.

"ANY BONDS TODAY." A two-minute animation short directed by Bob Clampett. It was shown in movie theatres across the United States to raise money for War Bonds during World War II. Animated by Virgil Ross, Bob McKimson, and Rod Scribner. Voice was that of Mel Blanc, music was by Carl W. Stalling, and editing was by Treg Brown. © Warner Bros. Entertainment, Inc.

## CHUCK JONES

On one of my first days at Leon Schlesinger's, a few of us were talking on our lunch break when Ruthie Pierce pointed to some men who were standing out in the hall talking. She said, "See that tall blond fellow, that's Chuck Jones. He became an animator when he was only twenty-one." Since Ruthie had worked there a few years and was an experienced painter, I was duly impressed.

Cartoons were always screened for us, after which we were to write a critique on each one. I noticed that quite a few had credited Chuck Jones as the animator.

As I have mentioned, Bob Clampett and Chuck Jones were sent to the Ub Iwerks Studio for a couple of months. Soon after their return, Bob was made a director and, a few months after that, Chuck was also given the opportunity to direct. His first cartoon was a Merrie Melodie in color, called "The Night Watchman." The main character is Tommy Cat. Tommy's father is too ill to do his job as a night watchman in a kitchen and appeals to his little son, Tommy Cat, to fill in for him. Tommy agrees to do the job but is no match for the larger rats who invade his territory. Tommy changes his tactics, though, and wins out in the end.

At Schlesinger's, we had an in-house newspaper, "The Exposure Sheet," that we published twice a month. An article in one of the issues was entitled "And They Call It Research!!" It continues:

> Due to the unusual backgrounds and customs in the new series of Canyon Kiddies Cartoons, James Swinnerton, Chuck Jones, and his story unit, left yesterday morning for the old Indian ruins of Arizona.
>
> Mr. Schlesinger felt that it was quite necessary for the department to be familiar with the general atmosphere of the country.
>
> They took a 16 mm. camera with which to capture, in color, the Indian dances, settings, and characters. They expect to gather enough material on the old Indian legends for the entire series of cartoons. (Have you ever heard of a cartoon studio going out on location?)
>
> P.S.—Tex Avery's story unit swear their next picture will have a Hawaiian background!!!

From "Exposure Sheet," Vol. 1, No. 4, "The Natives Return":

> The C. Jones unit's trip to Arizona for research on "The Canyon Kiddies" was a huge success, their one disappointment being their inability to secure many pictures of the Indians who thought the boys were taking a part of their lives when they snapped any pictures.

Chuck Jones and Martha at his Corona Del Mar gallery at the opening of a new exhibit. Photo by Shel Dorf.

Lobby card for "Old Glory." Released July 1, 1939. Patriotic cartoon directed by Chuck Jones, animation by Bob McKimson, musical direction by Carl W. Stalling, arrangements by Milton Franklin. Uncle Sam, voiced by John Deering, teaches Porky Pig the reason for the Pledge of Allegiance to the flag of the United States. © Warner Bros. Entertainment, Inc.

> On approaching the Indian settlement of Hoteavilla, they had a feeling of being in Shangri La because of the detachment and unreality of the place. And although it was almost zero weather, many of the old Indians walked around barefoot.
>
> In one hogan they saw a little old woman of 110 sitting near a stove, and were told she had been there for ten years, getting up only occassionally during the summer. The different tribes' manner of living were also noted.
>
> The boys were very fortunate in witnessing the ancient Bean Dance which only a hundred or so white men have ever seen, particularly as it may be the last time the Indians will have danced it. The leaders of the dance were all over a hundred years old, and almost blind. One was totally blind.

Sometime during 1939, all of us were made aware that we would be working on a very special cartoon, a patriotic picture entitled "Old Glory," directed by Chuck Jones, which carried with it a lesson in American history. The main character was Porky Pig, but there were also "Uncle Sam," Paul Revere, and the Minutemen. The thing that made this one cartoon different from all those done previously was that so many different tones of colored inks were used to produce shadows. For example, Uncle Sam had different shades on his hat, his beard, his face, and his clothes. Porky and all the other characters were done in the same manner. There were many cels of the American flag with its stars and stripes. There was so much more footage in this picture that its running time became nine minutes instead of the usual six or seven. Quite a bit of the animation was rotoscoped from a 1938 Warner Bros. live-action short titled "The Declaration of Independence."

As I have already stated, we were told right from the start that this was a very special cartoon and that we were to take great care with the way we painted it.

As fate would have it, Los Angeles was having a heat wave. It was over one hundred degrees in the studio. We had no such thing as air conditioning. There were two large fans, one at either end of the room, but they had to be aimed at the ceiling so that they didn't blow our cels and drawings all over the place.

It was decided that we would work at night until the heat wave passed. The temperature dropped about ten degrees at night and we were, somehow, able to finish the picture.

Until this one, all the Leon Schlesinger cartoons were first screened at the Warner Bros. Theatre on Hollywood Boulevard. This one, however, was scheduled to be previewed at the Carthay Circle Theatre. At the time, this was the most prestigious movie theatre in town.

All of our studio employees were invited to attend, in addition to the public. Many of us met at the studio and carpooled across town to the theatre. "Old Glory" was great and the audience loved it. All of us were extremely proud to have had a part in the making of it. The quality of this picture made Chuck a top-notch director in our eyes.

The main feature that evening was a Warner Bros. picture entitled "Dark Victory," with Bette Davis playing the lead. It, too, was terrific. This was a great night for all of us.

From "Exposure Sheet," Vol. 1, No. 13, "Old Glory":

> Raves have been pouring in from all over the country for "OLD GLORY." Trade papers, magazines, etc., have all been giving it more than favorable reviews.
>
> In Chicago, on the (July) 4th, "OLD GLORY" opened in two downtown theatres simultaneously, and then in ten neighborhood theatres. A great many women's clubs and organizations have endorsed the picture, and, as you know, these organizations have a great deal to say about the type of pictures to be shown where children and censorship are concerned. Long may 'OLD GLORY' wave!

Even though we enjoyed our work and the people we worked with, our salaries were very low. Most of us worked for the same salary year after year. Our inbetweeners, assistants, and a few of the animators decided to join other studio employees in forming a union.

My supervisor, Art Goble, said to me, "Martha, why don't you come to one of our union meetings?" I did, and found that many of our inkers and painters were there also. These meetings went on for

a few years, but nothing ever really happened. Then we became affil-
iated with the studio painters and carpenters.

Chuck became very involved and was responsible for getting the
animators, layout men, and background people to join in. Two other
directors, Frank Tashlin and Bob Clampett, also became involved in
our struggle.

Leon Schlesinger started making the animators take cuts in salary,
which, as you can understand, caused them to worry about the
future. So they joined us, too. We now had almost 100 percent of the
Schlesinger employees. Chuck definitely had done the most to get
our studio organized.

We found out that the MGM cartoon studio had already signed a
union contract, without a lot of problems. This encouraged us to
forge ahead. Herb Sorrell, who, I think, was the business agent for the
painters and carpenters, was negotiating for us, too.

Mr. Schlesinger called us down to the projection room and spoke
for a few minutes on how he could not increase our salaries due to
his budget. Then he turned the meeting over to his attorney, who
proceeded to insult us as if we had some nerve joining a union and
wanting more money and better conditions. This had a tremendous
uniting effect on us. We held a meeting at union headquarters, and
Chuck gave us an inspiring pep talk.

Negotiations broke down, and we decided to go on strike. It was a
scary time for all of us, as it was still depression days. The day we
were to strike, Leon Schlesinger locked us out. In its way, this was a
great thing for us, for, if we had gone on strike, we would not have
been eligible for unemployment insurance pay. Being locked out
gave us that eligibility. The lockout, however, lasted only a few days,
for Leon agreed to the contract and we were all called back to work.

A "side" story to this happened one day fairly recently when my
husband, Sol, who is a complete novice when it comes to the computer, was trying to surf the Web. And, surprise, surprise. Up came a
picture of me standing against the wall of the studio on the first day
of the lockout. Five of my fellow workers, Benny Washam, Roy
Laufenburger, a fellow whose name I can't recall, Sue Dalton, and
Paul Marron, were sitting on the front door step. Sol got so excited

and, after calling me to his side, transferred that excitement to me. I'm on the Internet now, though when that picture was taken, I couldn't possibly have conceived of either "computer" or "internet."

A Labor Management Committee was formed with representatives from each department. We each took turns serving on that committee. Chuck was the moderator. Incidentally, and this is of extreme importance in my feelings about Chuck, he couldn't be a member of the union, as he was considered a supervisor. I knew that eventually we would have a union, but Chuck was instrumental in getting it a lot sooner.

I left the studio in 1943, but I know that Chuck went on to direct many great cartoons with the help of his very talented unit and other members of the studio.

After Chuck left Warner Bros. and became a producer, some of his cartoons were inked and painted by Celine Miles, for whom I was working at the time. We did the "The Bugs Bunny/Road Runner" movie and "A Connecticut Rabbit in King Arthur's Court."

When Sol and I became docents at the Warner Bros. Museum in 1996, we would see Chuck on special occasions, one of them being the lavish party Warner Bros. threw for Chuck's eighty-fifth birthday in 1997.

Sol and I came home on the afternoon of February 22, 2002, to find a very sad message from Jerry Beck on our answering machine to the effect that Chuck Jones had died earlier that day. Even though we knew Chuck had not been in good health, we were very shocked and upset. To us, Chuck's passing was the end of an era.

Chuck Jones had a very good life and accomplished so much. He became world renowned as an animator, director, and producer of many fabulously funny cartoons.

Tributes from all over the world and throughout our country poured in by radio, television, newspapers, and national magazines. *Animation Magazine*'s April 2002 issue included an insert of a beautiful memorial booklet. In this tribute, there were remembrances by his wife, Marian; daughter, Linda Clough; Joe Adamson, author and film historian; Eric Goldberg, supervisoring director of animation; Stephen Fossati, executive producer/director of Chuck Jones's "Timber Wolf"; Jerry Beck, author and animation historian; Charles Carney, Warner Bros. book editor; and myself. This memorial booklet was compiled and edited by the capable hands of Ron Barbagallo.

On March 20, 2002, Warner Bros. held a memorial tribute to Chuck on their Burbank lot for over five hundred people in their Steven J. Ross Theatre. Some of Chuck's popular cartoons were interspersed with segments of Chuck and former colleagues speaking about his life in animation.

John Schulman, executive vice president of Warner Bros., was master of ceremonies. Family speakers were Chuck's wife, his daughter, and his grandchildren. Others were Leonard Maltin, Charles Solomon, June Foray, Eric Goldberg, Rob Minkoff, Roger Mayer, and Barry Meyer, CEO of Warner Bros.

After this very impressive program, everyone was invited to a buffet supper just outside the theatre. Chuck would have been so happy by the way this whole tribute was conceived and carried out. People came from all over the country to honor him.

On a personal note, many of my relatives, friends, neighbors, and acquaintances told me that when they heard the bad news about Chuck Jones, they thought about me. I took this as a real compliment as someone who knew, worked with, and admired Chuck for so many years.

## FRIZ FRELENG

Isadore was his real first name. However, since everyone at the studio called him "Friz," I assumed that this nickname came from the combination of the first two letters of his last name and the last two letters of his first name. Wrong!

Years later, I was talking with our friend, Larry Silverman, an animator who had worked with Friz in the Harman-Ising days. He told me there was a newspaper cartoon character by the name of "Frizby," and Isadore resembled him so much that the guys at Harman-Ising tagged him "Friz," and the name stuck. I'm sure he preferred "Friz" to his real name.

Friz Freleng, Martha, and Tom Ray at the Marina Fine Arts Gallery on the occasion of Friz's booksigning of *The Animation Art of Friz Freleng*. Photo by Michael Woolsey.

Friz came out to Los Angeles from Kansas City and worked for Disney and later for Charles Mintz in New York. In 1929, when Hugh Harman and Rudy Ising decided to go on their own and make a test film for their cartoon character "Bosko," Friz was one of the men who went with them.

When Leon Schlesinger decided that he would produce the series, Friz was the top animator, and his name appears on the first Looney Tune, "Sinkin' in the Bathtub." Not only did he animate, but he did story and layouts as well.

When Hugh and Rudy left Schlesinger's, Friz went with them, but he returned a short time later and became one of the directors. His first cartoon, released in 1934, was "Buddy, the Gob."

When I went to work at Schlesinger's in 1936, Friz was considered the senior director. Music was his forte, and this fit in perfectly with

Warner Bros., which had urged Schlesinger to use songs from the Warner feature films in the cartoons. Many cartoons in the early days did this. In fact, some cartoons were based entirely on the songs. Warner Bros. wanted the additional publicity for their songs. The more publicity, the more the public would buy the music.

Friz had the reputation of being a tough taskmaster, but he and his unit produced top-notch cartoons.

Other great cartoons that I liked from those days were "A Star Is Hatched," "Coo Coo Nut Grove," "She Was an Acrobat's Daughter," "Rhapsody in Rivets," "The Fella with a Fiddle," "You Ought to Be in Pictures," and my very favorite at that time, "Pigs in a Polka."

I enjoy seeing "The Fella with a Fiddle" over and over again because the complexity of it makes me realize now how very difficult it was for the inkers and painters to work on it. This cartoon was made in 1937. Here is a description of it, for those who haven't seen it, and I hope you can understand why it was hard and time consuming to work on: A grandpa mouse teaches his grandchildren a lesson in greed. He tells them of a miserly and dishonest mouse who pretends he is blind, wears tattered clothes and dark glasses, plays a fiddle on a street corner, and collects money as a beggar.

At the end of the day, he goes home to his shack in a junk yard, but as soon as he closes the door, he is in a beautiful mansion. He removes his beggar's clothing and dons a tuxedo. He has a butler who calls him "Master." He proceeds to his safe, where he removes lots of gold coins and enjoys tossing them in the air.

Suddenly, there is a loud knock at the door. He gets frightened and asks, "Who's there?" When the answer is "the tax collector," he panics. Alarms go off. He hurriedly runs around the room pushing buttons, and his luxurious furnishings flip backward, and his lovely home becomes an ugly hovel. Of course, when the tax collector enters, the miserly mouse is, once again, in his beggar's clothing.

The animators had to draw every minute step of transformation, and we had to trace and paint each and every cel. And, for this one sequence, there were hundreds. This process drove us all crazy, including Friz's sister, Lillian, who was a painter at that time. There was lots of swearing and complaining, but the finished product made the effort worthwhile.

Sometime in 1938, Friz received an offer from Fred Quimby at MGM that he couldn't refuse, so he left Schlesinger's. Although MGM doubled his salary, he was not happy there and returned to Schlesinger's a year later.

One of the first pictures Friz directed upon his return was a combination live action and animation with Porky Pig and Daffy Duck, "You Ought to Be in Pictures." In this classic cartoon, Daffy wants to be the only Looney Tune star. So he convinces Porky to try to get into feature films, where the money is much better. Porky sheepishly asks Leon Schlesinger to tear up his contract. Leon agrees, but when Porky leaves, Leon knowingly says, "He'll be back."

As soon as Porky leaves, Daffy Duck tries to sell Leon on the fact that he can fill Porky's job, and he does a song and dance to prove it. Leon reluctantly tells Daffy that he will think about it.

The live-action part of this cartoon uses some of our own studio employees as actors. Mike Maltese plays a security guard, complete with uniform. When Porky tries to drive into the motion picture studio, Mike angrily turns him away. Undaunted, Porky makes himself up to look like Oliver Hardy, the well-known comedian. Mike cheerfully lets him through!

Once inside the studio, Porky heads for the sound stage only to find the red light on. This he ignores, and enters anyhow. He observes a musical number in progress.

Gerry Chiniquy is the director, and others in the film crew are Henry Binder, Paul Marron, and Gladys Hallberg.

Porky is faced with an uncontrollable urge to sneeze. He sneezes so loudly and powerfully that he blows over a stack of film cans which make a huge, resounding noise. The director and staff are shocked because the entire shot has been ruined. They grab the culprit and eject him bodily.

Porky realizes he is not cut out for motion pictures and just wants to get back his job in cartoons. Sheepishly, he comes to Leon and asks for his old job. Leon tells him, "I knew you'd be back. I didn't tear up your contract. Now, go back to work."

He meets up with Daffy, who is still trying to get him to leave, but Porky beats him up badly. Daffy continues to con him and winds up with a ripe tomato in his face.

We all thought this was a great cartoon and that it was Friz's way of saying he was sorry he left us when he did. It was the studio's good fortune that he returned, for he went on to direct many terrific cartoons in his long career at Warner Bros.

## BEN ("BUGS") HARDAWAY

"Everything's up-to-date in Kansas City." So why, then, did so many Kansas Cityans, who once worked at the Kansas City Film Ad Service, namely Walt Disney, Ubbe Iwerks, Hugh Harman, Rudy Ising, Carmen Maxwell, Art Goble, Paul Smith, Melvin ("Tubby") Millar, Jack Miller, Ben Hardaway, Carl Stalling, and others come to Hollywood and try their luck in animated cartoons? Thank heaven, they did.

The Kansas City Film Ad Service seemed to be the springboard that landed many of those people in Los Angeles and into the cartoon business. Ben Hardaway was one of them, and, like most of them, he worked at Disney and Iwerks.

Friz Freleng had been hired as a director in 1934 at the new Leon Schlesinger studio and was given permission to hire people for his unit. As a result, he recruited Ben Hardaway and Melvin Millar as gagmen. Bugs contributed gags for about a year, until a chance to direct was offered to him. He directed seven Buddys, but as soon as Buddy was phased out, Ben went back to being a gagman.

The way I remember it, there were two story rooms. One was made up of the "Kansas City Boys," as they were called: Bugs Hardaway, Tubby Millar, Jack Miller, and a few others I don't recall. In the other story room were Tedd Pierce, Rich Hogan, Dave Monahan, and George Manuel. Mike Maltese and Warren Foster came later.

It wasn't until 1937 that storymen were given screen credit although this credit was rotated among all the storymen. Bugs Hardaway received screen credit for "Daffy Duck and Egghead" and "The Penguin Parade," both directed by Tex Avery.

Also that year, we were surprised when Friz Freleng left for what he thought would be greener pastures at MGM Cartoons. Needing someone to replace him, Leon chose Ben, as he had directorial experience.

I used to see Bugs during break time. I don't know why, but he would usually be standing in the doorway of his room. We had many conversations, for he was always very friendly to me. I had heard he was going to be directing, and I wished him luck. It was at this time that he told me he would be doing a Porky Pig hunting cartoon and that he was going to "put a rabbit suit on that duck." I got it, a character who would look like a rabbit, but have the crazy personality of Daffy Duck. A few months later, our department was painting a lot of scenes with a white rabbit. Soon after, "Porky's Hare Hunt" was shown in our projection room and received many laughs. I also saw that cartoon at the Warner Bros. Theatre in Hollywood and the audience just loved it. Of course, I reported this to Bugs the next time I saw him. He seemed pleased, but he never showed much emotion one way or the other. I think our studio was more than pleased however, because the publicity people at Warner's received lots of calls and letters from fans wanting to see more "of that rabbit."

Bugs and Cal Dalton, a longtime animator, teamed up to direct more than a dozen cartoons including another rabbit picture, "Hare-Um–Scare-Um." This picture also received accolades from the public.

One of Bugs's and Cal's cartoons that I really liked was "Hobo Gadget Band." This is a story about hobos and their carefree lifestyle. Throughout the picture, they utilized all kinds of clever gadgets and Rube Goldberg-type of contraptions. Their wanderlust drove them to the ever-passing freight trains. As soon as they heared the whistle, they rushed to board the train by sliding down a chute, and each hobo was catapulted into a separate freight car. Soon, they were singing and dancing and having a great time. When the engineer discovered them, he angrily brought the train to a sudden stop, as he pulled the "Hobo Eliminator" lever. All the hobos were ejected from the boxcars, and landed in a heap against a building. On the building was an ad from a radio station offering a prize for the best amateur musical group.

They made a mad dash for the radio station and, when next we see and hear them, they were playing their instruments which consisted of all sorts of homemade gadgets. They were so good that the master of ceremonies declared them the winner and presented them

Lobby card for "Hobo Gadget Band." Directed by Ben Hardaway and Cal Dalton, animation by Richard Bichenbach, musical direction by Carl W. Stalling. A group of hobos wins
an amateur musician's radio contest and receive a contract for musical appearances.
As soon as they hear the wail of a train whistle, they tear up the contract and run for
the tracks. © Warner Bros. Entertainment, Inc. Courtesy of Jerry Beck.

with the first prize. He offered them a contract promising them
wealth and luxury. The hobo leader signs his "X" on the contract
but, at that moment, they heard the wail and whistle of the freight
train. They rushed out the door to board the train. The leader returns
to the room and tears up the contract. As the cartoon ends, the master of ceremonies is shown looking woefully out the window and
watching the train disappear in the distance.

That was the plot of the story, but what made the picture beautiful were the backgrounds, the animation, the music, and the great sound effects.

Friz Freleng was not at all happy during the year he spent at MGM. So when Leon Schlesinger called him and asked him to come back, he did. Bugs went back to the story department, and Cal went back to animating.

Ben stayed only another year before he left to go to Walter Lantz, where he created Woody Woodpecker. Mel Blanc did the voice for a while until Leon insisted he sign an exclusive contract with our studio. Regrettably, I never saw Bugs Hardaway again but, many years later, when Bugs Bunny received his star on the Hollywood Walk of Fame, we were at the reception at C. C. Brown's ice cream parlor. It was here that I noticed a young man who resembled Bugs Hardaway so much that I had to go over to him and ask if he was related. He said, "Yes, I'm his son." We had such a nice talk, and I told him how much I had admired his father and related the story about "that rabbit" to him. He was so happy and appreciative and told me I had made his day. I also told him that I and others believed that the two rabbit cartoons his father directed were the forefathers of Bugs Bunny and there was no doubt that Bugs Bunny got his name from "Bugs" Hardaway.

It is of interest to note that Bugs Hardaway served in the U.S. Army for twenty-six months during World War One, with fourteen of those months being served in France with the Thirty-fifth Division, under the command of Harry S. Truman, who later became president of the United States.

## NORMAN McCABE

Norman McCabe's first chance to direct came in 1940. Prior to that, he was an animator in Bob Clampett's unit and received screen credit on many Looney Tunes. He eased into directing as co-director with Bob Clampett on two cartoons, "The Timid Torreador" and "Robinson Crusoe, Jr."

In 1941, Leon Schlesinger was expanding his staff and added another unit headed by Norm. From 1941 to 1943, he directed ten cartoons. His last was "Tokio Jokio." His screen credit listed him as "Corporal Norman McCabe," as he had enlisted in the U.S. Air Force and served in the first Motion Picture Unit located in Culver City, •California, at the Hal Roach Studios. It was given the nickname of "Fort Roach."

Norm continued working as an animator on training films. His commanding officer was Major Rudolph Ising. Norm must have felt right at home because he started his career in animation at Harman-Ising in 1932 as an inbetweener and progressed to an assistant animator. From there, he went on to being an animator, working for several years in that position, before being given the chance to direct.

Norm was an animator when I started working at Leon Schlesinger's. His wife, Fern, came to work there during World War II, in 1941, as a painter.

"Tokio Jokio" was released in May 1943. During the war, the studio produced cartoons that contained anti-Axis themes, which derided Germany, Italy, and Japan. This was in line with movies, radio, and newspaper reporting.

This particular cartoon shows a supposedly captured newsreel depicting life in Japan as far as fashions, sports, and home life. The story line and gags were fitting for that time in our history.

I left the studio in 1943 and didn't see Norm again for many years. I don't know if he ever directed cartoons again, but I know that he was animating at Warner Bros. in the mid-1960s and continued there until the 1990s.

# FRANK TASHLIN

Here today, gone tomorrow. Now you see him, now you don't. That was Frank Tashlin, who would be working at Leon Schlesinger's one day and, suddenly, gone the next day. He actually worked at Schlesinger's three different times. The first time, as I heard it, was in 1933.

Leon Schlesinger was in New York recruiting animators and gagmen, and Tash, who was working at Van Beuren Corporation in New York, was contacted by Leon and thought the job would be a golden opportunity. Frank Tashlin left New York and started as an animator and gagman in Hollywood.

That first stint didn't last too long, for Tash started a comic strip in a local newspaper and Leon thought he should have a cut of the money Tash was making from it. Tash refused and was fired, but he had no trouble finding work at the Iwerks studio.

However, when Leon needed another director, in 1936, he asked Tash to come back and head a unit. Tash returned, and the first cartoon he directed was "Porky's Poultry Plant," a Looney Tune in black and white. This happened to be the second picture that I worked on. When it was screened for us at the studio, we all thought it was just great.

I was too new in the business to appreciate how different it was, and I did not know that this was the first cartoon directed by Frank Tashlin. Looking at the quality of this cartoon now, I can really see how good it was for his first effort. Tash continued to put out excellent cartoons. He used all different kinds of camera angles, montages, and pan shots, vertical and horizontal.

From 1936 to 1938, Tash directed sixteen or seventeen cartoons and was making $150 a week. Then he had an argument with Henry Binder, our studio manager, and was gone again. He was hired at Disney as a gagman and then as a story director, at a salary of $50 a week!

I used to see Tash at union meetings, and I always asked him when he would be coming back to Schlesinger's. He said, "Oh, maybe someday," which he did—after a three-year absence. Tash was very pro-union, and when the Disney strike came along, he picketed along with all the others.

Before the strike, he was hired by Screen Gems, which was owned by Columbia Pictures, who distributed the Screen Gems cartoons. Tash ran the studio, and he hired many of the Disney strikers. Even though they were working, they spent many hours picketing and actively helping the cause of those on strike. They produced the "Fox and Crow" series and many others that cartoon historians believe were the best ever produced at that studio.

Things seemed to be going well and everyone there liked Tash. But the executives at Columbia and he had a difference of opinion about something, and Tash, once again, was fired. The whole studio protested by having a sit-down strike, which ended when Tash was called back to direct once again at Schlesingers.

I was so happy to see him again. Tash has been described as a "big bear of a man," but, to me, he was a teddy bear. He was so funny, so nice, and so talented and not at all pretentious. He didn't even have his own office. He did his work from a desk in the background department.

One of the pictures he directed after his third and final return was "Porky Pig's Feat," a very funny cartoon about Porky and Daffy, who are in a hotel and can't pay their room rent. The manager locks them in their room until they can pay. (How can you be locked in a room and be expected to come up with the rent? Only in a cartoon!) They try every which way to escape, but to no avail. Months later, they still can't get out and decide to call Bugs Bunny, hoping he can help them with their dilemma. Bugs, on the phone, questions them on each method they have already used in trying to get out. They said that they had tried them all. In the final scene, Bugs is shown in a room next door, also in chains, and he laments, "Don't work, do they?"

One of Tash's cartoons, "Puss 'n' Booty," has the dubious honor of being the last Looney Tune in black and white. However, many years later, this cartoon and many other Looney Tunes were sent to Korea to be colored. Personally, I wish they had never colored the black and white cartoons, because to me they were much better in their original form.

Tash directed "Swooner Crooner," which received a nomination from the Academy of Motion Picture Arts and Sciences in 1944. This cartoon has been written about in the magazine *Film History,* an international journal. This particular issue was entirely devoted to animation. Don Crafton, a professor of Theatre Arts at the University of Wisconsin at the time, wrote about it in an article called "The

View from Termite Terrace, Caricature and Parody in Warner Bros. Animation." "Swooner Crooner" is also on a videotape, among other Warner Bros. cartoons, entitled "Bugs and Daffy Wartime Cartoons, Rare Cartoons from Hollywood's Golden Age," narrated by Leonard Maltin.

Frank Tashlin, at Warner Bros., also directed several "Snafu" training films during World War II.

"Porky Pig's Feat," where Bugs Bunny had only a cameo role, "The Unruly Hare," and "Hare Remover," I believe, were the only times Tash directed Bugs Bunny cartoons. "Hare Remover" was the last cartoon for which he received credit at Warner Bros. The year was 1945.

Tash finished his cartoon directing career at Morey and Sutherland Productions. After that, he was able to achieve his real goal of writing and directing feature motion pictures. He also published three illustrated children books: "The Bear That Wasn't" (1946), "The Possum That Didn't" (1950), and "The World That Wasn't" (1951).

When I was working at the MGM cartoon unit, our back door opened on to Lot 2, which had many outdoor film sets. In 1948, Columbia Pictures rented one of those sets and shot *The Fuller Brush Man,* with Red Skelton. We saw Red every day, for he was such a friendly person, and even though that set was covered with tarps, he always came out during film breaks and handed out cigars and candy to everyone he met. His son had just been born and, understandably, Red was overjoyed. What I didn't know until the picture was finished was that Frank Tashlin was one of the writers.

Frank directed many films during his career and, in just about every one of them, he used cartoon gags. I guess animation never really left his blood.

On May 5, 1972, Frank Tashlin had a heart attack. He died three days later, leaving a devoted wife and young son.

## THE McKIMSONS

Whenever I heard the name Bob McKimson, it was followed by a phrase like "top animator," "best draftsman," or "fastest animator."

Leon Schlesinger made Bob McKimson head animator because of his great ability. Besides turning out a tremendous amount of footage, Bob would check the other animators to make sure they were keeping the characters consistent with the model sheets.

Bob and his brother Tom started their animation careers as inbetweeners at Disney and soon became animators. They didn't stay there long, however, but moved to Romer Grey's studio. Romer was the son of the well-known author Zane Grey. Romer put the McKimsons in charge of animation. This project was also short lived, and both brothers were hired at Harman-Ising as animators. They received many animation credits in their early days.

After Harman-Ising broke away from Schlesinger, Leon hired the McKimsons, among others, away from Harman-Ising. The brothers' careers flourished, especially Bob's. He worked in many units, such as Friz Freleng's, Chuck Jones's, Tex Avery's, and Bob Clampett's.

It was while he was in Tex's unit that Bob was given the job of redesigning the appearance of Bugs Bunny. Where previously Bugs's head was oval, Bob changed it to be more triangular and he seemed to make Bugs's facial features come alive. He also drew that classic pose of Bugs Bunny chewing on a carrot and leaning against a tree.

The McKimsons's younger brother, Charles, also joined the Leon Schlesinger animation staff. Chuck was very outgoing and fun loving, whereas Tom and Bob were genial but more serious.

In 1943, Bob did a new model sheet of Bugs Bunny. This was the most involved model sheet I have ever seen. Not only are there many full figures of Bugs in every pose, but there is a group of seven Bugs Bunny heads in each of those poses plus a myriad of facial expressions. This became a very famous model sheet, which served the studio for many years. Copies of this model sheet were made into plastic bags that were used in the Warner Bros. stores for customers to carry home their purchases.

Bob was also a top bowler on the men's team and a member of our mixed doubles bowling team.

I left Schlesinger's before Bob became a director, but I saw him from time to time when he brought work in to Celine Miles Ink and Paint while I was working there. I could not get over the fact that he never seemed to age. I often told him how great he looked. One day, I said, jokingly, "Bob, you must have a picture aging in your closet, a la Dorian Gray." He replied, "Oh, Martha, stop that. That's not true."

I was shocked and saddened a few years later when I heard that, while having lunch with Friz Freleng and others at the Smoke House in Burbank, Bob McKimson had a massive coronary and died right there. The year was 1977. Bob was only sixty-six. This was not only a terrible loss to his family and friends, but to all of animation.

Bob's brother Tom retired and lived to the ripe old age of ninety-four. Charles had his own business for a while and also brought work into Celine Miles, where I would see him. The last time we saw each other was when he and Bob McKimson Jr. were exhibiting their gallery cels at the Warner Bros. store in Costa Mesa, California, and my husband, Sol, and I happened to be there. It was wonderful seeing him again and we got a chance to talk briefly about the old days.

The McKimson brothers contributed much to the art of animation. Sadly, Chuck died at the age of eighty-four.

## VIRGIL ROSS

Virgil was one of the talented animators who was brought from Walter Lantz by Tex Avery when he came to Schlesinger's. He worked on all of Tex's pictures, starting at the old Termite Terrace on the Warner Bros. lot.

When Tex left Schlesinger's, Virgil became one of Friz Freleng's top animators. I remember particularly Virgil's animation of Bugs Bunny playing the piano in "Rhapsody Rabbit." It was a masterpiece.

Virgil said, "Every animator is like an actor, only he does his acting on paper." He felt he was too shy to be an actor and not good looking enough. In my opinion, Virgil's acting on paper, with all the personality he put into his animation, equals any great actor on stage or screen. Not only that, he was one of the nicest people I ever met in the cartoon business.

After Virgil retired, he got involved with creating drawings to be sold in galleries. He traveled all over the country to the various

Warner Bros. stores. When he made an appearance at the store in Santa Monica, California, some of us former "celmates" went to show our support. In our little group were Will Ryan, Tom Ray and his wife, Anna Lois, Jerry Beck, and Sol and I. We arrived early, but it was already a mob scene. People were lining up to meet Virgil and his wife, Frances, a former inker. His autographed framed cel pictures sold like hotcakes.

On the evening of the reception in Santa Monica, Virgil told us that he really loved doing that sort of thing. He enjoyed being picked up in a limo, being taken to the airport, flying all over the country, and meeting people from so many different places. Thankfully, he was able to do this for several more years.

When Virgil Ross died at the age of eighty-eight, Warner Bros. thought so much of him that they had a memorial reception for him on the studio lot. Many people attended, including Sol and I. The service was a beautiful and wonderful sendoff for a wonderful guy.

## PHIL MONROE

Phil Monroe started his long career in animation in 1934 at Leon Schlesinger Productions. Although he was an entry-level inbe-tweener, he was at that position only a short time when he was made an assistant animator. By the end of a year and a half, he became a full-fledged animator.

Phil was one of the most popular fellows in our studio. He was just as nice as he was good-looking and he had the most beautiful speaking voice. I told him one time that if he ever decided to leave the business, he could become a top radio announcer. In his most resonant voice, he said, "Not a chance, Martha."

His birthday fell on Halloween, and we always had a party for him. We all dressed in costumes. You can just imagine how creative these costumes were, made by cartoonists. Some were very risqué.

Phil organized our men's baseball team, which was part of an inter-studio league. Disney, MGM, and Screen Gems were members of that league. The games were played every Tuesday night during the summer at Griffith Park. Many of the fellows who didn't play and some of us girls were avid rooters for the team. It was great fun, and it gave us the opportunity to see some of our former colleagues who were now working at other studios.

On one occasion, the umpires didn't show up and the teams waited and waited for at least a half-hour but still they didn't show. Phil came to the stands and asked some of the men if they would be willing to umpire. A few tried and did so poorly that they were booed off the field. The stands started to empty out. Phil came over to me because he knew I had played baseball on the back lot at times with the fellows during our lunch break. I decided to give it a try in spite of the impending nightfall.

Manny Perez was the pitcher for our team that evening, and his ball was delivered so fast that I couldn't be sure if the ball was over the plate or not. I ventured a guess, and the remaining fans started to boo me. After a few more pitches, the game was called—much to my relief. I was kidded about this for the rest of the week and daily more cartoons appeared on the studio bulletin board showing caricatures of me try to umpire the game totally blind, praying for the game to end, and being burned at the stake, the stake being baseball bats.

Every year, the studio closed for two weeks of vacation. Phil and some of the fellows went to Catalina Island. Our first day back to work, the studio was all abuzz with the news that Phil had met a lovely young lady on Catalina and that they were already going steady. Her name was Beverly. All of us were so surprised for it all seemed so sudden. We thought so highly of Phil that all of us hoped it would be the real thing.

What seemed like a very short time later, Phil and Bev were married. They rented a little bungalow on Fernwood, which was the street on which I lived. Many times, as I was walking to work, Phil came out of his residence and we would walk just one block before we were joined by Treg Brown, and the three of us would continue on to the studio. By the time we had walked those three blocks, we had solved all the world's problems.

WHO WAS THAT SERGEANT I SEEN YOU OUTWIT LAST NIGHT?

PAT MATTHEWS

"Service Ribbin." Cartoonists from all the studios contributed gags to this magazine and they were distributed to all members in the Screen Cartoon Guild, including those in the armed services. The first one was printed in 1942. Martha Goldman Sigall Collection.

"Service Ribbin." This was the second edition, with Phil Monroe's picture on the cover, mailed in 1943. Martha Goldman Sigall Collection.

HOW ABOUT A LITTLE MORAL SUPPORT FOR THE TEAM?

Porky drawing, from "The Exposure Sheet." Porky is encouraging the employees to come out and support the baseball team. © Warner Bros. Entertainment, Inc.

Unfortunately, all our discussions went for naught for, on December 7, 1941, Japan attacked our country at Pearl Harbor and we were plunged into World War II.

Phil was classified 1-A and he knew he would shortly be drafted into the army. It was known that the air force was setting up the first Motion Picture Unit in Culver City, a small city surrounded by Los Angeles, to produce training films in live action and animation. Phil enlisted and was fortunate enough to be put into that unit. As time went by, many of the fellows from the cartoon studios enlisted and were assigned to this unit. They worked long hours, but they were able to go home at night.

Bev came to Leon Schlesinger's as an apprentice painter.

## MIKE MALTESE

Mike came to Schlesinger's as an assistant animator, from New York's Fleischer Studio. It wasn't long before he had everybody laughing so hard and so often that the bosses decided to put him into the story department. This was one of the best moves they ever made.

For a few years, he was in the story department "pool" of writers who contributed gags for all the units. Screen credit was rotated in the same manner as was the animators' credit.

It was decided later that it might be better if one storyman worked for one director, and Mike was selected by Chuck Jones. This combination turned out some of the funniest cartoons ever made.

A situation arose one day when Art Leonardi, an assistant animator at the time, told Mike he was so tired that he wished he could take a nap. Mike responded with, "We writers have it made. We have a couch in our room. I could take a nap and the bosses couldn't do a damn thing about it because I could always say I was deep in thought thinking about a story."

Mike has got to be one of the funniest guys I've ever known. We stayed friends all his life, until his death in 1980. Soon after, since he and his wife, Florrie, had been very, very close, I thought she might like to have a videotape of cartoons Mike had worked on and for which he had received screen credit.

At that time, there were seven cartoon shows on television each day that contained Merrie Melodies and Looney Tunes pictures. I taped them all and, as my collection grew, I would transfer the ones I didn't already have to the tape I was making for Florrie. I accumulated so many cartoons that I ended up giving her several tapes. Mike was given credit on over two hundred cartoons and, of course, I wasn't able to tape all of them. Florrie told me she appreciated them a great deal and that she watched them over and over.

As a result of making the tapes for Florrie, Sol suggested that since I had worked at Schlesinger's, wouldn't I like to have my own collection of Schlesinger and Warner Bros. cartoons?

From Jerry Beck and Will Friedwald's book, *Looney Tunes and Merrie Melodies,* which listed every cartoon made by Schlesinger and Warner Bros., and which I have used for years as a bible, I determined that Schlesinger and Warner Bros. produced 1,027 "Looney Tunes" and "Merrie Melodies" cartoons.

I was able to get more than nine hundred of these from television alone. Those considered politically incorrect and not shown any more were the ones I lacked. It was about this time that I first met Jerry Beck, and he was gracious enough to help me get quite a few of the ones I needed. Jerry also introduced me to Mark Kausler, who helped me get many more. I bought some from catalogs and video stores, and I now have every one of those 1,027 cartoons! It only took nine years to do!

## ARTHUR DAVIS

I knew Artie Davis before I even worked in the business. He and his dad lived in the same apartment building as my family did, the Welcome Arms, at 5617 Fernwood Avenue, Hollywood. I would see and speak with them many times in the short time they lived there.

It wasn't until I was at Schlesinger's and Artie came in to visit his old buddies that I learned he was an animator at Screen Gems. A few years later he joined our staff, in the same position, in Frank Tashlin's unit. I was now able to appreciate his ability as an animator and to get to know what a really nice guy he was.

After World War II, Artie became a director at Warner Bros. where he was responsible for more than twenty well-received cartoons. In fact, he directed the first "Goofy Gophers" cartoons with Mac 'n Tosh, and movie audiences just loved them. Artie directed only one Bugs Bunny, but it was a good one, "Bowery Bugs."

At one point, Warner Bros. decided to economize and cut out one unit. Since Artie's unit was the last added, his was the first cut. He went back to being an animator in the Friz Freleng unit, where he worked with other fabulous talents such as Hawley Pratt, who did the layouts; Irv Wyner, backgrounds; Warren Foster, story; and Virgil Ross, Gerry Chiniquy, Ken Champin, Manny Perez, Bob Matz, and Art Leonardi, animation.

This group worked on the Oscar winners, "Tweety Pie," "Speedy Gonzales," "Knighty Knight Bugs," and "Birds Anonymous." With Warren Foster in 1955, Artie co-wrote "Sandy Claws," which received a nomination for best cartoon. Artie was also credited as one of the animators.

Artie directed one more cartoon at Warner Bros., "Quackodile Tears," in 1962.

After Warner Bros. closed their cartoon unit, Artie directed cartoons at DePatie-Freleng, and I saw him periodically when I went there to pick up work to do at home.

Kansas City supplied the studios on the West Coast with many people who became prominent in our business. New York, though, sent us the biggest contingent, and Artie was one of them.

Arthur got his start as a very young man at Fleischer's. His brother, Mannie, was already an animator there. In the early days at Fleischer, the animators were given entire scenes to do. First, they would rough out all the extremes (main action), then go back to clean up those drawings, and fill in the action in between. This was a tedious, time-consuming process.

Fleischer thought it might speed up this process if another person assisted the animator. He asked Dick Huemer, a great animator even in those early days, to give it a try. At first, Dick refused because he was too fussy to allow anyone to touch his work. But, after thinking it over, he relented and picked Artie to assist him. Artie had the unique distinction of being the first "inbetweener" in the business, and he learned to animate from a master. The time frame for this event was somewhere in the mid-1920s.

Fleischer's was known for many innovations in animation. Among other things, the rotoscope was invented there. Fleischer's also created a new film series that was received very well by audiences all over the country. This live-action animated series was called "Song Car-Tunes." A famous singer would be photographed singing a very familiar song. Titles with the lyrics were flashed on the screen, and a bouncing white ball would move from word to word in time with the music. Here's how these clever people accomplished that feat: a round circle was drawn on white paper, cut out and pasted on a stick that was painted black. Artie was the one who moved the stick with a black-gloved hand and, since black on black does not photograph and is not visible, the audience saw only a bouncing ball moving in rhythm with the music.

I can remember going to the movies when I was a little kid in Buffalo, New York. My family and the audience enjoyed participating in this sing-along. I never thought, in my wildest dreams, that I would someday meet the person who bounced that ball.

Artie Davis was truly one of the great pioneers of the cartoon business. He lived to see a lot of progress and change take place. He died at the age of ninety-four, in the year 2000, leaving us with the memory of a very talented, admired, and respected man.

## PAUL JULIAN

Paul Julian came to Leon Schlesinger's in 1939 and was assigned to the background department. Even though background and layout people were extremely important in the making of cartoons, they received no screen credit until 1945. Paul and Hawley Pratt received their first screen credit for "Hare Trigger," which was also Yosemite Sam's first picture as the foil for Bugs Bunny. This picture is a classic as a result of the efforts of the people in the Friz Freleng unit.

Paul was also an accomplished pianist and, to add to his list of talents, he was an expert at handwriting analysis. The girls would some-

Lobby card for "Fast & Furry-ous." First cartoon of Road Runner and Wile E. Coyote; directed by Chuck Jones; story by Michael Maltese; animation by Ken Harris, Phil Monroe, and Ben Washam; layouts by Robert Gribboek; backgrounds by Peter Alverado; effects animation by A. C. Gamer; musical direction by Carl W. Stalling. Unaccredited "beep, beep" by Paul Julian. © Warner Bros. Entertainment, Inc. Courtesy of Jerry Beck.

times slip unidentified samples of their handwriting under his office door. He would post them on the bulletin board with his analysis beneath them. As far as we could tell, he was always "right-on."

I started taking handwriting samples to him of fellows I was dating, including one of Sol's letters from Guam, where he was stationed for a year and a half during World War II. In fact, I showed Paul's analysis to Sol even before I mentioned Paul's ability to him and asked him if he had any idea whose handwriting Paul was talking about. He immediately said, "That's me. It fits me to a 'T.'" In spite of that, I married him anyway, on April 7, 1946.

Paul's analysis went something like this: "This is a highly intelligent individual. A very quick learner and quite imaginative. He excels in mathematics and science, but not at all stuffy. He loves music. Was over-mothered, but not spoiled. He is as stubborn as people ever get, but if he is led to believe that something is his own idea, he will always be cheerful."

I don't know how many people know this about Paul. Mike Maltese told me that at the end of a working day, Paul would rush down the hall crowded with people on their way home. Paul was carrying oversized and heavy wooden background boards. He did his best not to bump into people but without much success. Instead of continuously saying, "Excuse me," he made sounds that seemed to be "Beep, beep. Beep, beep."

At the time, Chuck and Mike were working on a new cartoon with two new characters, the Road Runner and Wile E. Coyote. There wasn't going to be any dialogue in this picture, but Mike thought it might be good if the Road Runner, as he confronted and tormented the Coyote, kept saying, "Beep, beep." Chuck agreed, and asked Paul to do the voice-over. The cartoon was "Fast and Furry-ous," released in 1949. It wasn't until three years later that Chuck's unit made other Road Runner and Coyote pictures. But, in each and every one, the "Beep, beep" was that of Paul Julian. No screen credit was given though, since he was not a member of the Screen Actors Guild (SAG).

## MEL BLANC

Mel Blanc was known as "The Man of a Thousand Voices." Here is how Mel got into the business. He had come to Los Angeles from the state of Oregon and had been trying to break into the cartoon studios. As he did with all the other studios, he would come into Schlesinger's periodically seeking an audition. He was consistently

Late in his career, Mel Blanc made many public appearances at colleges and other organizations. He would hand out this autographed picture to members of the audience. A drawing of the cartoon characters was brought into Celine Miles's studio and after it was Xeroxed on a large cel, it was given to the author to paint. Elements under copyright of Warner Bros. Entertainment, Inc. Martha Goldman Sigall Collection.

told by Norman Spencer, the person who hired the voice actors, that the studio had all the voices it needed at that time.

One day in 1936, Mel came by and Treg Brown was filling in for Spencer, who was ill. Mel told Treg he would like to do some voices for him. Treg's response was, "Let's see what you can do." Mel did so well that Treg insisted the directors listen to him. Tex Avery asked if he could do a drunken bull, a character that he was going to use in a cartoon titled "Picador Porky." The bull was actually two tramps in a bull costume. Mel did the drunken tramp. The drunk sings "La Cucaracha." He was a smash hit with his interpretation, and the rest is history. Mel went on to be the voices of Bugs Bunny, Daffy, Tweety, Porky, Yosemite Sam, Foghorn Leghorn, Pepe LePew, Sylvester, and Speedy Gonzales. In later years, he appeared many times on the *Jack Benny Show* on television. Of course, this was preceded by his successful career on radio.

In 1961, Mel was involved in a serious automobile accident on what was then called "Dead Man's Curve," a portion of Sunset Boulevard in Los Angeles near UCLA. Almost every bone in Mel's body was broken. Rushed to the hospital, he was in a coma for several weeks.

One day, his doctor came in to his room to check on his condition and said, "How are you doing, Bugs Bunny?" In Bugs's voice, Mel answered. The doctor's question had brought him back to life. When Mel felt a bit better, a studio crew set up a small recording machine in his hospital room, and he actually did his voices for the cartoon characters in the cartoons then in production.

It is my understanding that, during the time he was unconscious, the studio advertised for someone who could duplicate his voice and that a line of people a block long tried out but not one even came close.

Mel's recovery was extensive and prolonged. He had to walk with a cane for a long time. Fortunately, he did recover and continued doing voices and went on a lecture tour of colleges across the country. Sol and I and some other "cartoon" friends went to see and hear his performance at Loyola Marymount University in Los Angeles.

Sadly, "that" voice was stilled in 1989.

# TREG BROWN

Treg's real name was Tregowith, but no one ever called him that. He was our film editor and sound effects man. He was a master at his craft and perfect at putting in unusual, creative sounds that made cartoons even funnier. He was greatly responsible for the success of the Schlesinger and Warner Bros. cartoons.

Tom Sito, then president of the Motion Picture Screen Cartoonists, Local 839, once interviewed the man who was the head of the sound department at Lucas Films. When Tom asked him who had influenced his work the most in the business, immediately, without even taking time to consider the question, he answered "Treg Brown."

Before entering the field of animation, Treg was a sound editor for Warner Bros. feature films. He was one of the first in the field of sound editing. Before getting involved in film, he was a member of the Red Nichols and His Five Pennies band, playing guitar and singing.

The studio was so lucky to have a sound man like Treg, who loved loud noises and utilized so many of them in the cartoons. One day, Treg walked by our painting room when we were still upstairs. It was very unusual for us, but it was so quiet in our room, you could hear a pin drop. As Treg walked by, he took notice of this and, at the top of his lungs, yelled, "Q U I—ET." He shattered the room's stillness. I wish I could tell you how many inkers' lines went haywire all over the cels!

This versatile guy, during his days in animation, would spend his evenings learning to be a chiropractor and we girls were the objects of his practice. Sitting all day, we really needed his expertise. Every time he walked by, one of us would call to him saying, "Me next."

After his graduation, he actually had an office where he practiced his trade, and I was one of his steady customers. Of course, this work was limited to his evenings. At first, he practiced at home and later opened an office on Sunset Boulevard where his wife, Mary, assisted him.

One time, when Warner Bros. closed their animation studio for a period of time, Treg went back to feature films. He was nominated and won the Academy Award for sound editing of the picture *The Great Race*. After having finished his work on this film, he moved to Spain but returned to accept his award.

Of all the wonderful people I worked with, I loved him the most. And I wasn't the only one who felt this way. Over the years, whenever I ran into anyone who had worked with Treg, they always commented on what a terrific person he was.

# CARL STALLING

Carl and I started at Leon Schlesinger's the same month, the same year, July 1936. As far as the cartoon business is concerned, the two of us were lucky to be in the right place, at the right time, twice. However, our commonality ended there. He was hired as a very talented musician/composer who had the experience of being the musical director both at Disney and Iwerks. I was hired as an apprentice painter. Enough said!

Carl started playing piano as a young child. According to our in-house newspaper, "The Exposure Sheet," his biography states that he played piano at a silent picture theatre starting at the age of fourteen. A few years later, he was conducting the orchestra and playing musical accompaniment at the Isis Theatre in Kansas City, Missouri.

This is where his first right place came into being. Of all the silent movie houses across the United States in the early twenties, and of all the thousands that had organists accompanying those movies, who would walk into the Isis Theatre and be so impressed with the style that this organist brought to his craft but a struggling producer of animated cartoons, a very young Walt Disney!

Carl had the ability to combine well-known music while improvising musical notes that he had composed. Walt introduced himself to Carl and they struck up an acquaintance. Carl arranged for the screening at the theatre of a couple of Disney cartoons and Carl played the accompaniment.

Their friendship continued by correspondence after Disney moved to California to start a new studio.

Before long, sound was on the horizon revolutionizing the movie and cartoon business. The Disney studio completed the animation for "Steamboat Willie," and Walt went to New York to record the sound and preview the picture. On his way, he stopped in Kansas City leaving two animated cartoons for Carl to write the music. When Carl was through, he joined Walt in New York to record them. Disney must have been pleased with the result because he offered Carl the position of musical director if Carl would move to California. Carl readily accepted for it was a great opportunity. He realized that, with the advent of sound, an organist in a silent movie theatre would soon be looking for a new career.

Carl worked for Walt Disney and completed almost twenty pictures before leaving that studio to join with Ub Iwerks, as his musical director, when Ub left to form his own studio. He stayed until the studio closed in 1936.

Carl wasn't unemployed long. He received a call from Leon Schlesinger who was looking to replace his then-current musical director. Ben Hardaway, a story- and gagman, who worked with Carl at Iwerks and was now back working at Schlesinger's, urged Leon to hire Carl, recommending him very highly. This was another smart move on Leon's part because Carl became an integral member of the team that would make the "Merrie Melodies" and "Looney Tunes" the tremendous success that they have enjoyed all of these years.

Music is an extremely important part of both feature films and cartoons. Music can set the whole mood necessary to the action. The directors and Carl had been told by Warner Bros. that they should use as much music as possible that had been popularized originally in Warner Bros. feature films. By so doing, the public could associate more closely with the cartoon and perhaps purchase more copies of the songs. It gave additional publicity to the Warner songs.

Like the musical directors before him, Carl had the entire Warner Bros. music library available to him plus the use of Leo Forbstein's fifty-piece orchestra. This was the second, the ultimate, right place for Carl.

We had heard how much the musicians in the orchestra enjoyed playing Carl's style of music. They would go from serious music on feature films to the happy-go-lucky style of Carl's.

Carl worked for Leon Schlesinger and, later, Warner Bros. for twenty-two years. He was credited with the music of more than five hundred cartoons. Milt Franklyn was Carl's arranger from the late thirties and did a fantastic job. The last few years of Carl's tenure, the two of them shared musical direction credit until Carl retired in 1958, and then Milt took over from him.

Carl was such a modest man. When people praised his work, he shrugged it off as just something he learned as an organist in the silent picture years. He died in 1971 at the age of eighty. He was a fine gentleman, and his contribution to the field of animation has been immeasurable.

## TEE HEE

His real name was Thornton Hee, but everyone who knew him called him Tee Hee. He was an animator and caricature artist. He drove a little Triumph automobile that was the apple of his eye. It was a convertible, and he always wore a beret when he drove it. Somehow, he always found a space right in front of the studio each day to park it.

One day, some of the fellows decided to have a little fun with him. They actually picked up the car and carried it through the front doors into one of the rooms in the studio. Came noon and lunch time. They waited eagerly for him to go out and look for his car. They saw him rush out—it was gone! He almost had cardiac arrest on the spot. He got so upset, but it wasn't until he was about to call the police that the fellows told him where the car was. They carried it outside and deposited it back into his parking space. What muscles!

Just prior to Christmas 1936, he made a caricature picture showing many of the men in the studio, and all of us received one as a Christmas card.

Caricatures of animation staff and front office drawn by Tee Hee and given to all Leon Schlesinger employees as a Christmas card, December 1936. *Top row, left to right:* Art Loomer, Phil Monroe, Nelson Demarest, Bob Clampett, John Burton, Carl Stalling, Volney White, Ralph Wolfe, Harold Soldinger. *Fourth row:* Louis Cavett, Paul Smith, Chuck Jones, Tom Baron, Jimmy Clabbe, Doc Scott, Norm McCabe, Ken Harris, Cal Dalton, Ray White. *Third row:* Ace Gamer, Irv Spector, Melvin ("Tubby") Millar. *Second row:* Smokey Garner, Al Freleng, Cal Howard, Ben ("Bugs") Hardaway, George Manuel, Frank Tashlin, Grif Jay. *Front row:* Tee Hee, Leon Schlesinger, Ray Katz, Henry Binder, Tex Avery, Friz Freleng (below Tex Avery). Martha Goldman Sigall Collection.

## BENNY WASHAM

Before Benny came to Schlesinger's, he was a partner with Bob Wein, who started Bob's Big Boy, the very popular and successful hamburger restaurant. Benny was the fry cook and since he was an artist, he designed the famous statue of the "Big Boy." He wanted to get into animation so badly that he left the partnership before it got so popular. If it had not been for animation, he probably would have ended up a millionaire.

He started for six dollars a week as an inbetweener, and in a month's time, received a raise to twelve dollars, and by the end of the year was up to twenty-five dollars. This was 1936, a month before I arrived.

He was always going into Mr. Schlesinger's office trying to get a raise and was always turned down by Mr. Schlesinger, who would ask, "Are you better than Ken Harris?" Benny always had to answer, "No." "Ken's always satisfied with what he's getting," Schlesinger would add. Benny would walk out dejected.

After this scene repeated itself over and over for about a year, Benny walked into Schlesinger's office again saying, "I demand a raise for Ken Harris!" When Ken found out about this, he was furious and told him to mind his own damn business.

## KEN HARRIS

In the early 1930s, Ken Harris was selling automobiles. But, how many cars could he sell during the depression? He wanted to break into the cartoon business in the worst way and tried desperately to find some-one who would allow him to come into the studio so he could learn animation. Week after week, he made the rounds of the studios, but no one would take him. He was persistent and kept making those rounds. Finally, it was Romer Grey who gave him his chance.

They made a deal whereby Ken would pay Romer, not the other way around, mind you, ten dollars a week. This was a lot of money in those days. But, week after week, Ken paid Romer his ten dollars.

After about six months, Ken was called into the office, told that they had been following his work very carefully, and that, if he kept improving, he would one day become one of the top animators in the business, which he did become. As a result, they wanted to give him a raise. From that time on, he could work for nothing!

Chuck Jones, one evening in the Warner Bros. Museum, told me that that wasn't the end of the story. As Chuck told it, when Ken got home that evening and entered his home through the front door, not knowing where his mother was, he ran in yelling, "Mom, Mom, they're going to let me work for NOTHING!"

The Schlesinger and Warner Bros. Merrie Melodies and Looney Tunes were produced by a team. It was a team effort from beginning to end. The people that I have singled out were just a part of that team. There were many other directors, storymen, layout designers, background artists, animators, assistants, inbetweeners, inkers, and painters, and the supervisors and checkers for each department, even cel washers and polishers, too numerous to mention by name, who did their bit in making these cartoons as successful as they became.

When these cartoons were being produced and exhibited, we had no idea of the lasting effect they would have. In those days, we felt that the cartoons would be shown all over the country and then fade into oblivion. We had no idea that some day there would be such a thing as television and that these cartoons would be reissued over and over again, and new ones would be made. Because of this exposure, we now have hundreds, maybe thousands, of animation historians, cartoon buffs, and collectors of animation.

There were very few of us who had the foresight to save drawings, cels, and so forth that were available to us once a picture was finished. In the early days, when I started in animation, celluloid (nitrate) cels were the only ones available. When the picture was finished and approved, the ink and paint was washed off and the cels were used over and over again, sometimes as many as six times. How could something like that, something that could be washed off and reused, be of any value? Little did we know. We could have had anything we wanted after the cartoon was completed. If we had kept our work from those days, we would all be millionaires now, and amply compensated for our low salaries.

# [ *chapter 7* ]

# TALES FROM
# TERMITE TERRACE

## THE WILLIE KING BOYCOTT

Willie King was not part of the crew at Leon Schlesinger's. Willie had a little lunch counter set up on the middle of the lot. He would sell Cokes and other goodies to the fellows and girls, much as I used to do for the men at Pacific Title when I was still in school.

The fellows on the second floor of the studio rigged up a pulley with a basket at its end so that Willie could get their food and drink to them more easily for him. But many times when he had the basket full, before he could begin pulling on the rope, the fellows on the first floor would reach out their window and swipe the contents. This and such other antics were probably responsible for making Willie a very angry person. He never was nice to any of us.

In anticipation of the large rush from the Schlesinger employees, he would always have the Coke bottles uncapped so that the people could take one, pay him his five cents, and be on their way. We had only a fifteen-minute break. At this time, there was a radio station, KFWB, located on the lot and Maxwell House Coffee had a production company there, rehearsing for a variety show. Willie, with this new flood of customers, raised his price for Coke to ten cents. Naturally, we objected. I suggested to everyone at Schlesinger's that we boycott him, and this is the way it worked.

Knowing that Willie would have all the bottles uncapped, we walked toward his stand en masse until we got to within about twenty-five feet of him, and then we stopped. We pretended to talk among ourselves for a few seconds, then turned and walked back to the studio. Willie, of course, saw what was going on. He got furious. He had all the Cokes opened for us, and we didn't buy any of them! He was stuck with all those full, uncapped bottles.

He was so infuriated that he went storming into Mr. Schlesinger's office and was told, "My kids can't afford to pay ten cents." His response was, "Well, I'll get them. They have no other place to go." He even threatened to raise the price to twenty-five cents.

The next day, Mr. Schlesinger sent me, since I was president of the Looney Tune Club, to the market nearby to buy Cokes for everyone. Cokes were very cheap the way I bought them in large quantities. The next day, Tex Avery bought them for everyone, then Chuck Jones, then Bob Clampett, and then Bob McKimson.

Knowing that this couldn't last, we contacted the Coca-Cola Company, which installed a Coke machine. This cost us nothing except the bottles of Coke themselves. Candy machines also were installed by the vending companies at no charge. The Looney Tune Club got all the profits, after paying for the merchandise. Mr. Schlesinger also gave the club all the commissions earned from the studio's pay telephones.

I have to explain that Coke machine. It was a long, rectangular metal cabinet filled with water kept cold by electricity. It was my job, as president of the club, to open the Coke bottles every day, and Dave Mitchell, the vice president, collected the five cents.

We had this machine for about a year when it was replaced by a slightly improved model.

Anyone wanting a Coke opened the lid of the machine, inserted his or her five cents into a coin slot, and the clamp holding the neck of the bottle would open, and the bottle could then be removed. A bottle opener was affixed to the machine.

Willie King boycott. When Willie doubled his prices, Schlesinger employees boycotted him, and Mr. Schlesinger bought cokes for everyone. Martha Goldman Sigall Collection.

Tex Avery was the biggest prankster of us all, and it didn't take him long to concoct something for this machine. With a number of his fellow employees watching, he opened the lid of the Coke machine, opened a bottle with a hand opener, put a straw into the bottle, and drank the whole thing. The bottle was still secured to the machine by the clamp holding its neck since Tex hadn't put in any money. He proceeded to fill the empty bottle with liquor and push the bottle cap back into place.

Everyone stood around waiting for the "victim" to appear. I think it was Gil Turner. He put his money in, grabbed the bottle, and started to gulp the Coke as though he were going to drink it in one swallow. Needless to say, he was so shocked that the contents in his mouth went spraying out five feet across the room. Everyone just howled.

1. Martha clinking bottles with 2. Tedd Pierce 3. Raynelle Bell 4. Dave Monahan 5. Irv Spector 6. Keith Darling 7. Sid Sutherland 8. Rudy Zingler 9. Ruth Pierce 10. Rudy Larriva 11. Fred Jones 12. Volney White 13. Rev Chaney 14. Manuel Perez 15. Frances Garcia 16. Charlotte Darling 17. Olga Rogers 18. Mildred O'Blenis 19. Betty Burke 20. Richard Thompson 21. Jay Gould 22. Irven Spence 23. Lee Halpern 24. Hank ("Smoky") Garner 25. Melvin ("Tubby") Millar 26. Art Loomer 27. Ana-Lee Camp 28. Werdna Benning 29. Shirley Bromberg Kahn 30. Lois Waggonner 31. Mabel Andes 32. Betty Brenon 33. Carmen Del Mar 34. Murray Hudson 35. Paul Marron 36. Rich Hogan 37. George Manuel 38. Eleanor Minett 39. Frances Bacon 40. Richard Williams 41. Rod Scribner 42. Phil Monroe 43. Mildred ("Dixie") Mankameyer 44. Virgil Ross 45. Frank Powers 46. Gerry Chiniquy 47. Louis Cavett 48. Ace Gamer 49. Margaret Fellger.

## RAIDED

Every day after we finished lunch, we would rush back to the studio, usually about twenty minutes to one, with work resuming at 1:00 P.M., to play showdown poker. Each player would put a nickel in the pot, all the cards were dealt face up, and the best hand won. Almost every day, Tex Avery, just before the sound of the "go back to work" bell, would say, "Let's make these last few hands a dime." So the pot got a little bigger. There was no skill involved. There were usually eight to ten of us who played, including Mr. Schlesinger. Maybe it was just luck, but I seemed to win a few dollars each week. We had a lot of fun.

One of the girls thought it was so disgusting that we would "gamble" every day that she called the police. She was one of the inkers and, for the most part, was a loner. She ignored everybody and she, in turn, was ignored. When the police arrived, about 12:30, they were too early. There were only two guys playing, and there was just ten cents in the pot. In walked the police, and the fellows were told, "You can't put any money on the table. That is gambling, and gambling is not allowed. This has got to stop." They went into Mr. Schlesinger's office and told him. Having no alternative, Mr. Schlesinger announced the inevitable, "I hate to do this to you kids. I know you have a lot of fun, but what can I do? The cops stopped it." For about two or three months, we didn't play, but the girl who had complained soon left the studio and we gradually started once again.

The fellows didn't always play just showdown poker. Other types of card games were also played. One day, Tex Avery lost ten dollars to Mr. Schlesinger and didn't have the money to pay him. A couple of days later, Leon said to Tex, "Hey, Tex, you owe me ten dollars. When are you going to pay me?" Tex said, "I'll pay you as soon as I get paid. O.K.?" So, what did Tex do? He got ten dollars worth of pennies and dumped them all on Schlesinger's desk and walked out.

A similar thing happened when Chuck Jones owed Leon five dollars. When Schlesinger asked for his money, Chuck paid him off with five dollars worth of pennies—in a jar of honey.

Another debt repayment involved five dollars loaned by Tedd Pierce, one of our storymen, to Benny Washam, who promised to repay him in a few days. Even before the week was out, Tedd started needling him and was told by Washam, "You'll get your dough with interest yet." The next day, Benny handed Tedd a home-made loaf of bread with five hundred pennies baked inside!

# EVERYTHING IN ITS PLACE

One of the fellows in the studio was very fastidious. He had a place for everything, and when it was time for him to go home at the end of the day, he would open his desk drawer to ensure that each pencil, each pen, each eraser, et cetera, et cetera, was in its place. Only then would he lock the drawer. To my knowledge, he was the only one in the whole studio who locked his desk.

He was the kind of guy who wore a hat, both summer and winter. One summer day, he came walking into the studio wearing a white Panama hat that he had bought on sale from a hat store on Hollywood Boulevard. They had even put his initials on the inside hatband. This went along very nicely with the white shirt, tie, and jacket he always wore. He thought he looked great, and he did, especially beside the other fellows who wore jeans or other casual clothes.

One day, the fellows decided to have some fun with him, and they went up to the same hat store and bought two hats identical to his, even had his initials put into the hatbands. The only difference between these and the one he had bought was that one was smaller and the other larger. At this point, I'm afraid you're already ahead of me!

When he wasn't looking, the fellows removed his hat and substituted the one that was too large. Just about going-home time, the fellows gathered in places where they could watch him but not have him get suspicious. They watched as he opened his desk drawer, ensuring everything was in its place; they watched as he locked his desk; they watched as he put on his jacket and then the hat. It came down over his ears! He held it at arm's length with a disbelieving look on his face. He tried it again and again, and each time it continued to come down over his ears. He checked the hatband and found his initials there. It had to be his hat, but how had it gotten so large? He couldn't comprehend! He stuffed some animation paper inside the hatband, put the hat on at a jaunty angle, and walked out as fast as he could so that no one would notice. Oh, no?

The next day, he came into the studio with that same hat, and again at that jaunty angle. During the day, when he wasn't at his desk, the fellows changed hats again, putting the smaller one on top of his jacket. Again, with everyone looking without his knowledge, when it was time to go home, he checked his drawer and locked his desk. He put on his jacket, looked at the hat casually, and put it on. It sat on the top of his head! What's going on? He looked at the hatband. His initials were still there. It had to be his hat, but how did it get from being too large to being too small? He just couldn't figure this one out. It never occurred to him that the fellows might be pulling a gag on him. Again, out he walked as fast as he could, with the hat at a slightly different jaunty angle.

The following day, the fellows told him he had been had, and they gave him back his original hat. It wasn't until then that he realized what had been going on.

## NUDITY

During the hot spells, and on this particular day, the temperature had to be over one hundred degrees in the studio. We didn't have any air conditioning or fans. We just suffered.

Gil Turner decided to take off all his clothes down to his shorts. He even took off his shoes and socks, and he scotch taped animation paper to his feet so as not to get any splinters. He sat there in his little cubicle, in this state of undress, doing his work. One of the fellows noticed that Gil had his clothes hanging on the partition that separated his cubicle from the next. Here was the prime opportunity for more fun! He went into Henry Binder's office. Henry was our office manager. Pretty soon, his voice came over the loud speaker, "Would Gil Turner please come to Henry Binder's office."

Gil got very panicky. He turned around to get his clothes. Gone! He knew the fellows, at least some of them, were responsible. But who, and what had they done with his clothes? He got very upset. He started cursing and yelling at all the guys. He pleaded with them for his clothes, but they all played dumb.

Five minutes later, the same loud speaker blared, "Will Gil Turner please come to Henry Binder's office, immediately." Gil ran around the room in his shorts looking into everyone's cubicle, every cubby-hole, with the fellows still pretending they didn't know what was going on. Gil was having fits.

"Gil Turner, come to Henry Binder's office NOW." Gil is now screaming at the guys, "Give me my clothes, give me my clothes." They did, and he got dressed as he ran down the hall to Henry Binder's office. He opened the door and said, "You wanted to see me, Henry?" Henry replies with, "Go back to work, Gil. It was just a gag."

## HOW TO DOUBLE YOUR SALARY

In 1939 or 1940, when Murray Hudson was an assistant animator, making twenty-five dollars a week, he got the idea to raffle off his paycheck. He sold fifty chances at one dollar a chance. He would try to sell as many as he could, but never fewer than fifty. You don't have to do much mathematics to realize that this resulted in a gain to him of at least twenty-five dollars. Murray would try this every two or three weeks!

## AN ASSISTANT ANIMATOR'S MOMENT OF GLORY

Earlier, I told the story of how Bugs Bunny got his name. Now I will relate the story of how Speedy Gonzales got his. This happened long after I left Schlesinger's in 1943. The studio was sold to Warner Bros. in 1944. The naming of Speedy took place in 1953, and I didn't know about it until 1997, but I now have it in writing from "the horse's mouth."

The assistant animators were told they would have to do a minimum of forty breakdowns (drawings) a day. As a way of rebelling, they got together and decided they would do no more than forty a day.

One of these assistants, Frank Gonzales, always came down to the story room about four o'clock each day. Quitting time was 5:30. One afternoon, he came into the story room where Tedd Pierce and oth-

Lobby card for "Speedy Gonzales." Academy Award winning cartoon of 1955. Directed by Friz Freleng; story by Warren Foster; animation by Gerry Chiniquy, Ted Bonnicksen, and Art Davis; layouts by Hawley Pratt; backgrounds by Irv Wyner; voice characterization by Mel Blanc; music by Carl W. Stalling. © Warner Bros. Entertainment, Inc. Courtesy of Jerry Beck.

ers were working. One of the men asked him, "Frank, how come you're always down here about four o'clock just to shoot the breeze?" He answered, "Well, you know, all of us decided that we would do forty breakdowns, but no more. I figured out a way to speed up my drawings." Tedd shouted excitedly, "That's it! Speedy Gonzales, the fastest mouse in all Mexico."

Tedd had been working on a picture called "Cat-Tails for Two," but he didn't have a name for the main character. It was the first picture featuring Speedy Gonzales.

Tedd took Frank's hand and said, "Frank, I'm going to take you out to lunch tomorrow." And he did.

I have known Frank and Colene Gonzales since 1946. Frank was an inbetweener, and Colene was an inker at MGM when I worked there. Frank went on to be an animator and layout man. He and Colene have retired in Dolan Springs, Arizona, and we still keep in touch. Neither Frank nor Colene ever mentioned this story to me and, in 1997, I heard it for the first time from Tom Sito.

I couldn't believe that I had known the Gonzaleses for so long and they had never mentioned the story to me. I wrote to Frank and asked him if it was true. Frank wrote me back, in detail, as I've given it to you. I guess I'll save his letter forever.

# NEPOTISM

Ray Katz was Leon Schlesinger's brother-in-law and worked at the studio as production manager. He always wore rubber soles on his shoes so that he could walk up behind you, without your even being aware of his presence, to see what you were doing. The fellows complained about it, but he persisted. Ray never said anything to anyone, never asked any questions about the work that was being done.

Every morning at 10:30, he would come into the ink and paint department, and open the double doors on a tall cabinet in which we kept all the finished scenes. He never touched anything, but just stood back a couple of feet, eyes fixed on the open cabinet, and rocked on his heels for two or three minutes. He would then close the doors and walk out without ever saying anything to anyone. Knowing that he would show up at 10:30, everyone would always be quiet as a mouse at that time.

I got the idea to pull a gag on him. Let's empty all the scenes from the cabinet, put them on top of our desks until he left, and see what happens. Right on the dot of 10:30, in walked Ray Katz. He opened the two doors of the empty cabinet, moved back a couple of feet, and stood rocking back and forth on his heals looking at that emptiness for his usual two to three minutes, closed the doors, and without saying anything to anyone, walked out. We didn't know if we had had him or he had had us!

When an animator is working, he will put three or four finished drawings between his fingers and flip them to make sure the action is smooth. Also, when the animators received a finished scene back from his assistants and inbetweeners, he would also flip the drawings to ascertain that the action was smooth. Ray Katz had seen the animators do this, but never asked why. Did he know or didn't he? Therein lies this tale.

Ray once walked into the music department and saw a stack of music piled on one of the desks and very nonchalantly walked over and started flipping them. When finished, he grunted something under his breath, apparently giving approval, and walked out of the room.

From that day on, whenever Ray went into the music department, they handed him the music sheets for him to flip.

## BLOWUP

An excerpt from the May 27, 1940, issue of "The Exposure Sheet" read: "Have you heard the Bing Crosby blow-up? It's quite rizzgay!"

Someone in the recording studio was able to get hold of the recording Bing was making and on which he flubbed his lyrics. The songs were "Jimmy Valentine" and "Wrap Your Troubles in Dreams." At the point of forgetting the correct lyrics, Bing didn't stop and start over again, but kept right on singing the music and making swear words to fit in. Copies were made and sold throughout the studio for one dollar. I still have mine and wish I had bought more. Of all the Crosby songs over so many years, I am positive that if this one had gotten out to the general public, it would have been one of the biggest hits of his career.

## ANNIVERSARY CONGRATULATIONS

On June 10, 1940, "The Exposure Sheet" extended congratulations: "Yesterday marked the thirty-first wedding anniversary of Mr. and Mrs. Schlesinger, and we would all like to congratulate them and wish them many more years of happy married life."

# [ *chapter 8* ]

# THE INK AND PAINT DEPARTMENT

What is the most important thing animation cartoon painters needed to do their job? The obvious answer, of course, is the paint. Grumbacher, an art supply firm, sold paint to Schlesinger's and to most of the other cartoon studios, with the exception of Disney, which made its own.

We needed a wide range of colors. That's easy to understand. But we also needed different shades of all of those colors to compensate for one or more cels being placed on top of each other. Four cel levels were used in each scene throughout the picture. Because each cel has a density that changes the color or colors under it, we had to compensate for that density by using a different shade of that color or by using a blank cel.

It is a little involved but let me try to explain that last paragraph. It was a given in our studio that four cel levels (four cels placed one on top of another) would be used in every cartoon in order to ensure that the density of each frame would be consistent throughout the cartoon. For example, if only one character was animated through-out a particular scene, three blank cels were used along with the one on which the character appeared. If two characters on separate cels were reacting to each other, then only two blank cels were used to maintain the density.

This paint had to be especially suited to be used on nitrate cels. It came in all basic colors, in large sixteen-ounce jars. Our studio bought these colors and then added white to make as many as twenty shades of each basic color.

Ann Almond, who was Betty Brenon's sister, handled this time-consuming and tedious job. She would take a large amount of one of the basic colors and pour it in a big bowl and add a small amount of white. Then, she would paint a swatch on a cel and, when it was dry, check to see if the mixed paint compensated exactly. She would pour some of this mixture in a dozen or so small jars and label the new shade, for example, "Blue 19." She would continue adding white until she had all the shades down to "Blue 1." "Blue 20" was the basic color. All the paint jars were labeled with the color and number. I wondered why she was hardly ever in a good mood. Now I can understand.

We needed to use many shades of gray, as the Looney Tunes were still done completely in black and white, using the paint created through the process just described, but starting with the darkest gray. Every time Ann mixed a new batch, she would label each jar with a letter of the alphabet. A slightly different shade of each letter was labeled with that letter and with 1-½. The darkest gray I can remember was H-½; the lightest gray was B.

Shades of white needed to be compensated, too. So Ann mixed white with gray and labeled them Wh, ½, A, A½. These were the whites.

The Grumbacher paint had its drawbacks. In wet and cold weather, it would stay very sticky. Even after the scenes were finished and the paint seemed to be dry, we might hear the final paint checker shrieking that the paint was sticking to the drawing. We would try to avoid this by using our little corn starch bags to dust the cel. We made these bags by pouring a small amount of corn starch on a paint rag and tying it with a rubber band.

We also used "slip" cels to put between the finished painted cel and the drawing. A "slip" cel was one that had the ink and paint

washed off so many times that it couldn't be used in production anymore. These cels also helped to prevent the paint from cracking off
when the weather was hot. We put these "slip" cels between the
newly painted cel and the drawing only after the paint had dried.

Another objection to Grumbacher paint was that it didn't stay
fresh. Sometimes we would open a jar, and the paint would be slimy
and have a terrible odor. Because of these deficiencies, we struggled
with it until sometime around 1938, when the studio started dealing
with another paint manufacturer, Catalina Color Company, owned
by Edgar Wilkerson. His product was so much better. The colors came
already blended. Ann didn't have to mix one basic color into twenty
shades. The grays now were labeled numerically from one to twenty.

Ed was up in our department quite a bit, listening to all our com-
plaints and made a strong effort to keep improving his paint. He was
very friendly and seemed to like us, and we liked him. He seemed
smitten with our Ruthie Pierce and they dated quite a bit. In 1940,
however, when war clouds were on the horizon, Ed, who had been a
lieutenant colonel in the Army Reserve, was called into the regular
army. How we, and especially Ruthie, hated to see him go.

Hiram Mankin, Ed's chief chemist, now had to take over Ed's job.
Of course, this didn't include Ruthie. "Hi" did his best to help us
with our paint problems.

At the end of World War II, I heard that Ed no longer wanted to
continue in the paint business. "Hi" then became the owner and
renamed it "Cartoon Colour Co.," located in Culver City.

Hi is part of a family that goes way back to the early days of the
cartoon business. His brother-in-law was "Max" Maxwell, a real pio-
neer with Disney, Harman-Ising, and MGM. His sister-in-law, Janice
Holloman, started as an inker in 1928. His son, Hiram Jr., was an
inbetweener when I was at MGM and became an animator and layout man at Hanna-Barbera. Currently, Cartoon Colour is owned by
Hi's granddaughter, Patti Griffith, and her husband, Van.

Since I lived in Culver City, my employers would frequently ask
me to pick up paint on my way to work. As a result, I have had a lot
of contact with all the generations of the Mankin family. The nitrate

cels gave way to plastic acetate around the late 1950s, but we still call them cels, even today.

A new company called Spectacolor sprang up and began creating an acrylic paint that was better suited to the new plastic cels. Dick Thomas, a Warner Bros. background artist, had an interest in this company. For a while, Cartoon Colour lost a lot of their studio customers to this new venture, but Hi got very busy and also perfected an acrylic paint that he called "cel vinyl." No doubt, it was a better product, for he gradually got most of the studio business back.

Cartoon Colour also supplies cels, brushes, ink, and just about everything a cartoon studio needs. Even though computers have replaced the need for paint and cels, Cartoon Colour still has customers throughout the world.

# [ *chapter 9* ]

# THE INK AND PAINT GALS

Much has been written and said by other authors about those in the animation hierarchy, the producers, the directors, the animators. Very little light has been shown on those beneath them, those who comprised the biggest portion of the team.

I probably have mentioned previously the way I felt when I started working in an animation studio. I could not believe how lucky I was to have a job painting animated cartoons. I kept thinking I should pinch myself to see if it was real. "I'm painting cartoons and getting paid, too!" All of $12.75 a week!

Most of the people in the studio were great fun to be around. I use the word "most," because there is always someone in every group who would like to make your life miserable. But, the way I remember those days, there was always a fun thing going on.

One of the nicest people was Ruthie Pierce, whom I have already mentioned. She was someone who was sweet and helpful to everyone, including the newcomers. She had been painting at the studio for three years when I arrived, and I could tell that everyone was very fond of her.

Three of us were hired the same day, Mary Lane, Gladys Hallberg, and I. Mary Lane was very tall, pretty, friendly, and always serious about her job.

Gladys had had some experience at Disney. Soon she was given the job of painting shadows. After a scene is completed, if a character had a drawn shadow underneath him, it was usually outlined in blue pencil by the animation department. The paint was a transparent gray mixture. As soon as it was painted on the cel, it had to be blotted dry with a piece of toilet paper.

Personally, I would have found this boring, but Gladys did this day in and day out and received three dollars a week more than a regular painter.

Several months later, she became a final checker, and this paid ten dollars a week more. She held this job until she left the studio in 1943. She was a fun person and she and her husband, Bill, gave a lot of terrific parties. She was involved in everything that was going on socially at the studio. Unfortunately, she died a few years after leaving the studio.

The first month after I started as an apprentice painter, I was very nervous. I concentrated on doing my work without making mistakes. I was the youngest girl there, for one thing, and every week I worried I would be fired because I didn't think I was fast enough with the work. Most of the girls in the department were very friendly with one another. Some were even friendly toward me. Even so, I felt like a stranger in a strange new land.

In August 1936, two new inkers were hired. One of them looked familiar to me. Her name was Raynelle Bell, a girl I had known from Hollywood High School. Although she was a senior when I was a sophomore, we both went out for softball and were teammates. After she graduated, I did not see her again until she came into our department. I was happy to see a familiar face, and over the years, we became good friends.

Raynelle worked at the studio about a year when Max Fleischer moved his studio from New York City to Miami, Florida, where he was going to produce a full-length feature, "Gulliver's Travels." A few adventurous people, Cal Howard, Tedd Pierce, Dave Monahan, Raynelle, and a few others, left Schlesinger's to join the Fleischer group in Miami.

It was there that Raynelle met her future husband, Frank Day, while attending church. When the picture was finished, most of these people came back to Schlesinger's. One of the nice things about Leon was that he was willing to hire back people who had left him previously. Raynelle was one of those who returned and continued to worked there for quite a few years.

In 1960, when I was looking for work to do at home, I heard that Raynelle was the ink and paint supervisor at Snowball, Bob Clampett's studio. She gave me work immediately. In those days, none of us needed a resumé. Most experienced cartoonists knew one another and the quality of each person's work, and we had this great network. Whenever I went to a new studio, I always ran into people I knew, a fact that made working in this business so much more pleasurable.

We worked on the Beany and Cecil series, but that lasted only two years, then all of us had to look for new jobs. Several years later, I met up with Raynelle at Kurtz and Friends. When Raynelle retired, she lived in Eugene, Oregon, to be near her son and daughter. She passed on in November 2002.

During my first few months, I was aware of a discussion among the girls that seemed to go on from day to day. The subject was the coming election, Franklin D. Roosevelt's bid for a second term. Each day, the same person, Frances Bacon, would start the conversation going by speaking with each of the girls individually. Her position was that Governor Alf Landon, the Republican standard bearer, would garner the same number of electoral votes as Roosevelt, so that the choice would have to be made by the members of the House of Representatives.

No one agreed with her, not even the few girls who were planning to vote Republican. Frances was from Alabama and had a very heavy southern accent. And when she said it would be a tie, it sounded as though she were saying, "It's going to be a 'tah.'" We heard that word over and over again. Most of the girls argued with her in no uncertain terms. But being very new there and not being of voting age, I wouldn't get into any argument with her.

As election day drew near, she just would not let up. You would think that the election could be decided by our girls in the ink and paint department! In fact, she was so sure of her theory that she proposed a bet: if Roosevelt won, she would bring in a five-pound box of See's candies. However, if it ended in a "tah," the girls who thought otherwise would have to bring in a five-pound box of See's for her.

Frances was not able to get any of the girls to her way of thinking. Even the Republican girls argued that it wouldn't end in a "tie." Jackie Langdon, Sue Gordon, and I were not of voting age and couldn't be part of this bet, but this did make the election a little more exciting for us.

Roosevelt won the election handily. Governor Landon only won two states, Maine and Vermont, with a total of just eight electoral votes. He didn't even carry his home state of Kansas.

The next morning, Frances's desk was covered with headlines from the morning papers. You can imagine her mood. She was very quiet and very sad to think that her estimate of the election was so far off. But she was a good sport and brought in the candy on the following day.

Among the other people I remember in our department is Mabel Andes. She was one of the first painters hired when the studio opened. She was a widow with two teenage boys but was always cheerful and in good humor. She was already in her late forties and had made up her mind that when she reached fifty, she would retire. When she did, we made a big party for her.

We would have a party at the drop of a hat. If one of the girls was going to get married, we had a party for her. There was a party for almost any holiday. There were parties for no reason at all. Outside of our work, parties were our second priority. And they were always fun.

Another popular painter was Auril Blunt. Don't let that last name fool you. She wasn't Blunt very long, just about a year, for she married Dick Thompson, who later became a well-known animator.

Auril was a fine artist in her own right. She progressed from painter to inker and then on to the special effects department as an assistant to Ace Gamer. All the special effects that you see in

Schlesinger and Warner Bros. cartoons through 1953 were painted by Auril. They were used as stock shots for years to come.

Auril went on to have her own ink and paint service. She is retired now, living in the San Diego area, and we remain the best of friends.

Another member of our crew was Dixie Mankameyer. She, too, married someone in the business, a longtime animator by the name of Paul Smith. Dixie was one of those always arranging parties, especially theme parties such as scavenger hunts, treasure hunts, "come as your favorite slogan," and others. Besides being very socially inclined, she was one of our fastest painters. There was no one who didn't like her. We remained good friends until her death in the early 1990s.

Shirley Bromberg was also an excellent painter. She was another of the girls who married a fellow in the business. Her husband was Milton Kahn, known to us in the studio as David Mitchell, which was the name he used during the short time he was in motion pictures. Sol and I had been very close friends with them for many years until Dave died in 1999. Shirley continued to be one of our best friends until her untimely death on April 18, 2001.

Add to this group Peggi Morgan, who later married Bob Matz, an animator. Prior to their marriage, during World War II, Peggi joined the WAVES and Bob went into the U.S. Navy. Upon their return home at the end of the war, they married. Both were in the business a long time and continued to be close friends of ours. Bob died on March 8, 2003.

An interesting article from "The Exposure Sheet," Vol. 2, No. 4, dated March 4, 1940, gave the following tidbits of interest:

**THE ALL-SCHLESINGER GIRL should have:**

Dixie's eyes

Dawn's nose

Lee's mouth

Helen's complexion

Jackie's hair

Gladys' personality—and legs

Ruthie's disposition
Bobbie's poise
Mabel's sense of humor
Auril's sweetness
Sue's daintiness
Frances G's neatness
Betty B's appeal
Eleanor Speere's figure
Frankie's intelligence
Hazel's patience

And
Martha's tonsils

# [ *chapter 10* ]

# WORKING CONDITIONS

The Leon Schlesinger studio had once been a warehouse as part of the old Warner Bros. studio. Its floors were very porous. One day, Ruthie Pierce, one of our painters, accidentally spilled her paint water, and unbeknown to us, it trickled down to the floor below. Gil Turner, one of the nicest guys in this world, was working on a three-foot-long panoramic drawing filled with birds. Ruthie's black paint water had gone through the floor and landed right on his drawing. He rushed up the stairs to our room with a look of complete disbelief on his face and holding the ruined drawing in his outstretched arms. His face was all red; he was livid. His mouth was open, but words refused to come out. While horrible, the scene was also so funny that we burst into laughter. We just couldn't help ourselves.

The drawing that Gil was working on was what we call a "stock shot," meaning that it could be used over and over again in different cartoons whenever needed. When we later recognized this scene in various pictures, we would start laughing again in memory of how it all started.

The floors of the ink and paint department were so shaky that whenever anyone walked across the room, the inkers would scream as their desks shook and their ink lines ran all across the cel. They would scream loudly at the culprit. We all tried to remember to walk very softly, but sometimes we just forgot.

At times, the girls could be as bad as the fellows. In one of the storage closets that had been used by the film studio, there were life-sized dummies that had been used in the making of motion pictures. One day, when I returned to work from lunch, one of these dummies was occupying my place at my desk, wearing my smock, and holding a paintbrush in its hand. It was not unusual to open the door to the ladies' room and find one of the dummies sitting on the toilet.

A gag the girls always played on a new inker, including me, was this: when that new girl left her desk, for whatever reason, they would take a cel that they had previously inked with big splotches of black ink all over it, put it on top of a cel the girl had finished inking and had left on her pegboard, so that it appeared as though the black ink had spilled all over her cel. When she returned, we usually heard a loud shriek from the girl, who was now badly shaken and scared. Don't blame this one on me, I never got involved—in this one.

Helen Cope was one of my best friends at the studio even though she was a dyed-in-the-wool Republican and I was a staunch Democrat. During one of President Roosevelt's campaigns for reelection, someone pasted Roosevelt bumper stickers all over Helen's desk. She immediately thought I was the guilty party and accused me of it. These stickers were almost impossible to remove and remained on her desk for a long time. It wasn't until about three years later, when Suzie Williams left on maternity leave, that she confessed she had been the culprit. For all those three years, Helen had been convinced that I was the one responsible in spite of my protestations.

Milton Kahn, aka David Mitchell, got a job contributing gags for our cartoons, but unfortunately he wasn't able to draw. And a storyman needed to be able to draw gags for the storyboard. He did other odd jobs around the studio, but he wasn't paid anything. Every week, he was fired! Why? I don't really know. But every Monday morning, he was rehired. This went on for several months until Tedd Pierce said to Henry Binder, "Why don't you give the guy ten bucks a week?

This guy is here every day doing things. Why don't you pay him something?" They did. He stayed there for a couple of years, and by the time he left, he was making twenty-five dollars.

Dave was hired as a writer for Jerry Fairbanks on the series "Speaking of Animals." He stayed there until he went into the service during World War II. During the war, he was stationed in Honolulu with Armed Forces Radio as a writer. When the war ended, he got a civilian job with them in Los Angeles and remained there in that capacity until he retired.

# chapter 11

# STUDIO ROMANCES

When people worked and played as closely as we did, it was just natural that a lot of friendships would turn to romance. Virgil Ross married an inker, Frances Ewing; Paul Smith married Dixie Mankameyer; Dick Thompson married Auril Blunt; Dave Mitchell married Shirley Bromberg; Bob Matz married Peggi Morgan; Paul Marron married Charlotte Langdon; Murray Hudson married Lee Hathaway; and Cal Dalton married Sue Gee. Harold Soldinger dated Dawn Smith, but it didn't result in marriage. When I first started at the studio, there was a married couple, Fred and Virginia Jones, already there. Two other couples whose wives came to work at the studio after marriage were Norm McCabe and his wife, Fern, and Phil Monroe and his wife, Beverly.

As the girls got engaged, we always had showers for them and a great time was had by all. When Shirley Bromberg got engaged, we were all told to bring canned goods to the shower. She got a tremendous amount that looked like a six-month supply, at least. However, one of the hostesses, I think it was Virginia Morgan, without Shirley's knowledge, removed all the can labels. There were small cans, there were large cans, but nothing to identify the contents. You can imagine the meals she and Dave must have had during the early days of their marriage. Can't you see them shaking the cans, smelling the cans, trying to determine their contents!

We even had a shower for one of the fellows, Frank Powers, who was supervisor of the ink and paint department after Art Goble left. It was a surprise shower, and we did it on our lunch hour. When the bell rang at twelve o'clock, we watched as he started to get up from his desk to go to lunch, and all the girls pounced on him. He was shocked. We had brought all kinds of food and gifts. We even arranged for his fiancee to show up and join in the festivites. It was all very hilarious.

# STUDIO PARTIES

As I've mentioned previously, being the fun-loving group we were, we were always having parties of one type or another. At one of the "Come as Your Favorite Slogan" parties, most people came with ordinary costumes from ordinary slogans, but there was one fellow, whom I prefer not to name, who came dressed as a condom. The slogan, written in large letters at the bottom, stated "To Be Used in the Prevention of Diseases Only." Can you imagine? And this was after just his first week in the studio! He was isolated at the party. No one went near him.

The best parties, however, were the Christmas parties Mr. Schlesinger threw for the employees. They were always for lunch, all you could eat and drink, at a popular nightclub, the Wilshire Bowl on Wilshire Boulevard near Fairfax. There was even an orchestra for dancing. During World War II, he even gave everyone a savings bond.

One year at Christmastime, when we arrived at the studio at 8:30 in the morning, the early birds were already partying. A crap table had been set up and was in full use by the fellows and Mr. Schlesinger. Others were playing cards or standing around "shooting the breeze." Liquor was already flowing. There was something going on in every room. It's a good thing the cops didn't raid us that day! At about 11 A.M., we all started heading for the projection room,

Leon Schlesinger

Invites you to a

Christmas Luncheon

To be held at the

Wilshire Bowl

5665 Wilshire Boulevard

On Saturday, December 23rd

At 12 Noon

R.S.V.P.

Kindly present this
invitation at the door

Christmas party invitations. Every year, Leon Schlesinger treated all of his employees to a Christmas party. © Warner Bros. Entertainment, Inc. Martha Goldman Sigall Collection.

Leon Schlesinger

invites you to a

Christmas Luncheon

to be held at the

Wilshire Bowl

5665 Wilshire Boulevard

on Saturday, December 24th

at 12 Noon

Kindly present this invitation
at the door.

R.S.V.P.

Christmas party invitations. © Warner Bros. Entertainment, Inc.

where "blow-ups" and out-takes from the Warner Bros. feature films were shown. They were simply hilarious and added greatly to the already festive mood. During 1939 and 1940, we made movies of our own, showing people from the studio in various gag situations, and these, too, were shown for our enjoyment.

Then we carpooled and headed for the Wilshire Bowl. Even though this was for lunch, the party didn't end with the food. We didn't actually leave the Bowl until about five o'clock, and then a bunch of us drove out to Gladys Hallberg's home in the Valley, where the party lasted until the wee hours.

By midnight, everyone was ravenously hungry again. Gladys brought out eggs and bread and proceeded to make "one-eye" sand-wiches. Never heard of a "one-eye" sandwich? Until then, neither had I.

Want the recipe? Take a shot glass, use it as a cookie cutter and make a hole in the middle of a slice of bread. Butter the top side of the bread and place it in a hot, buttered, frying pan. Crack open an egg and drop the contents into the hole. Let it cook until congealed, turn it over for a few minutes. We devoured dozens of these. When our two boys were small, I made these for them frequently. Our son, Bobby, at about the age of two, couldn't say, "one-eye" and called it "eye-why." This name stuck, and our grandchildren wanted "eye-why's" when they were small.

Unfortunately, 1941 was the last year we had these parties at the Hallbergs. With the beginning of World War II, Bill Hallberg and most of the fellows in all the studios enlisted in the armed forces. Schlesinger continued with the Christmas parties each year, but they weren't the same. It was wartime, many of the fellows were in the various services, the atmosphere was entirely different.

During a winter weekend, probably in 1939 or 1940, a whole bunch of people from the studio, with their wives and husbands, rented a bus and went to the snow at Big Bear, in the San Bernardino Mountains.

On their return trip, the bus driver lost control of the bus on the icy road, went over the side of the mountain and, fortunately, hit a large tree that kept the bus from crashing to the bottom of the

Schlesinger employees at Big Bear, a resort in the San Bernardino Mountains outside of Los Angeles. *Left to right:* Jack Carr, Paul Smith, Dave Mitchell, Mildred Mankameyer, Henry Binder. Martha Goldman Sigall Collection.

At Big Bear, *left to right:* Ada Ruinello, Dave Mitchell, Tex Avery, Friz and Lily Freleng, Ginger and Virginia Morgan, Mrs. Cal Dalton, Ruth Pierce, Bob Givens, Chuck and Dorothy Jones, Herman Cohen, Paul Smith. *Back to camera:* Pat Avery telling everyone when another bus will come to pick them up. Martha Goldman Sigall Collection.

"What we need is an animator who can shoot 35,000 on the marble machine and play left field on our baseball team .. by the way, can you bowl?"

APPLICANT

CARTOONS

Henry Binder, from "The Exposure Sheet." Caricature of Henry Binder interviewing a prospective employee. © Warner Bros. Entertainment, Inc. Martha Goldman Sigall Collection.

ravine. People were shaken up, but unhurt. The exit doors were jammed, however, and no one could get out.

Resourceful Tex Avery kicked out the rear window, and everyone was able to climb out. Included in this group were Friz Freleng and his wife, Lily; Chuck Jones and his wife, Dorothy; Paul Smith and Dixie Mankameyer; Bob Givens; Ginger Morgan and her husband; Cal Dalton and his wife; Dave Mitchell; Gladys Hallberg; Ruth Pierce; Henry Binder; Herman Cohen; Jack Carr; and Tex Avery and his wife, Pat. Considering the contributions made by these people in the years following, can you imagine the loss to the cartoon industry if the bus had careened to the bottom of the mountain?

Our bowling team was always trying to find ways to raise money to cover team expenses. One day, we came up with a dandy: we raffled off Herman Cohen! We sold chances for ten cents apiece. If memory serves me, we made about five dollars. But the raffle was fixed, and everyone knew it except Mabel Andes, who was in her fifties, our oldest painter, but a great gal with a great sense of humor.

The mixed doubles bowling team of 1941. *Top row, left to right:* Harold Soldinger, Ray Bloss, Paul Callier, Lew Irwin, Dave Mitchell, Art Heineman, Henry Binder, Bob McKimson, Herman Cohen. *Front row:* Dawn Smith Benedict, Martha Goldman Sigall, Frances Garcia, Lillian Heineman, Mildred Mankameyer Smith, Billie Lee Jackson, Shirley Bromberg Kahn, Virginia Lee, Helen Cope Berg, Ada Ruinello Nickelad. © Warner Bros. Entertainment, Inc. Martha Goldman Sigall Collection.

When we drew her name, she was so thrilled, for she loved Herman, as all of us did. He came into the room, we handed each of them an ice cream cone, and he sat on her lap. I know pictures were taken, but I have no idea where they may be today.

The girls on the bowling team also raised money by making sandwiches which they brought into the studio and sold for ten cents apiece. We tried to out-do each other as to the type of sandwich and, as a result, ended with onion sandwiches, bean sandwiches, and so on. Someone even brought in a chop suey sandwich.

During football season, we always had a "pool" going in the studio every week. For baseball, we had a pool for the World Series. For boxing, we had a pool for every heavyweight fight.

In football, I had my own "pool." Each year, for the Rose Bowl game, I would buy four tickets, raffle off two of them, selling enough chances to pay for all four tickets. That way, I was able to treat my then-boyfriend to the Rose Bowl game for free. That was my Christmas present to him every year.

# STUDIO ACTIVITIES

Bowling was mostly a men's sport and had been around for many years. However, in the late 1930s, it became very popular as a co-ed sport. Bowling alleys sprang up throughout the Los Angeles area and all around the country.

I became involved in the sport at a bowling alley on Vine Street, between Sunset Boulevard and Hollywood Boulevard. As one entered the building, there was a bar and lounge where the King Cole Trio entertained nightly. Nat King Cole played piano and sang with his sweet and velvety tones. His voice and his personality were captivating. This was a number of years before he became so well known, selling millions of albums.

My friends from the studio and I bowled there until the Sunset Bowling Center opened with fifty-two lanes. The building was formerly occupied by Warner Bros. main office. It stretched an entire block on Sunset Boulevard in Hollywood. It was the largest bowling alley in the country, containing a restaurant, a bar, men's and ladies' dressing rooms with lockers, and comfortable theatre seats for spectators.

Our studio people lost no time in frequenting these lanes on our lunch break and after working hours. The price was twenty-five cents a line.

Mr. Schlesinger decided to sponsor both men's and women's teams. The fellows were the "Looney Tunes" and the girls, the "Mer-

Caricature of Leon Schlesinger, from "The Exposure Sheet." © Warner Bros. Entertainment, Inc. Martha Goldman Sigall Collection.

rie Melodies." He had pants and monogrammed tops made for us girls and monogrammed shirts made for the fellows.

He and his wife came to watch us when they could. After our league play finished for the night, he would bowl with some of the fellows. He was a darned good bowler.

One Sunday afternoon, the Sunset Bowling Center held a fundraising event to aid England with their war effort. It was called "Bowling for Britain." The sponsors of all the teams donated a large sum of money. Admission was charged for spectators and almost every seat was filled. Many movie stars attended, some of whom came over to Mr. Schlesinger. He introduced us to them as "his kids."

An English actor was one of the people who approached Mr. Schlesinger and we were again introduced as "his kids." When the English director Mr. Fleming came by, the English actor introduced him to Mr. Schlesinger and, referring to us, said, "These are his children."

In 1941, the two teams were combined into one and joined a mixed-doubles league. This all came to a halt the following year when the fellows left to join the armed forces.

## "SKETCH PAD VARIETIES"

In 1938 and again in 1939, the people working at Schlesinger's wrote little skits that they put together into a stage presentation for which they charged their families and friends twenty-five cents admission. This money was used to fill up food baskets for the needy people at Christmastime with Schlesinger donating a ham or a turkey for each of the baskets.

The playbill for 1938, which was printed on a small piece of folded gray paper, said, on its front page, "The Schlesinger Club Presents 'The Sketch Pad,' Friday Evening, April 21st." The top of the inside page read, "Addresses by Mr. Schlesinger and Dave Monahan."

The back page was blank.

The following excerpts from "The Exposure Sheet" applauded this performance:

> In a blaze of glory, amid the fanfare of trumpets and the huzzas of an enthralled audience, the Schlesinger Dramatic Club presented the "Sketch Pad"—first edition—to inaugurate a new dramatic season.
>
> The show was opened by a thrilling trumpet duet. The instruments were manned by two moppets named, so the program said, Billie Lee and Frances Garcia. Lacking more reliable authority, we will have to take the program's word for it—though they jolly well didn't look like Billie Lee and Frances Garcia in those livid, beet-like get-ups. At any rate, they could and did trumpet in a very stirring manner.
>
> They were immediately followed by Mr. David Monahan, the boy tenor of Dana Point, who gave a brilliant and flowered speech on "The Story Man's Place

in Modern Society." Mr. Monahan never seemed in better voice, and when he made his graceful exit, the audience stayed in its seat as one man.

Following this, came a quiet little talk by Mr. Leon Schlesinger. This gentleman complimented the group on the hard work and time they had spent, and failed utterly to mention that he had donated quite a chunk of company time and personnel in order to insure the success of the venture. He also somehow neglected to mention that it was through his influence that the group were able to secure the cooperation of the Western Costume Co., KFWB, and Warner Bros. Incidentals, no doubt, hardly worth mentioning.

This was followed by a short description of each play and accolades to some of the cast members. The final paragraph is worthy of mention:

At this time, it would be nice to mention the man behind the flats: Johnny Burton, who is always called upon at the eleventh hour and never fails to deliver. It might also be of interest to everyone to know that when the tumult and the shouting had died, when the captains, kings, and the producers had departed—when the compliments and the paeans had died away, it was this same Johnny Burton who came down the next day—Saturday—and almost single-handed struck and stored away the scenery it had taken four men to erect.

These two comments were taken from the same edition of the paper:

In every stage production there are always a good many things that happen backstage that are a good deal funnier to the cast than any part of their act.

For instance, just five minutes before the sketch "On the Lot" was to go on Friday nite, Martha Goldman was talking to Harold. He noticed that after talking to him only a second or two, she hurried away seemingly a little pink around the ears. A few minutes later, Mitchell rushed over with a needle and thread to sew up a certain part of his costume. Five minutes before curtain!

Of course we had reports all day Friday how Martha Goldman kept rehearsing her one line, swallowing innumerable aspirins, and someone even caught her gargling just before 5:30!

*The*

*Schlesinger Club*

*Presents*

"THE SKETCH

PAD"

*Friday Evening, April 21st*

"Sketch Pad Varieties" of 1938. © Warner Bros. Entertainment, Inc. Martha Goldman Sigall Collection.

"Sketch Pad Varieties" of 1938. *Left to right:* the three members of the "Les Larson 'Rhythm Rascals,'" Herman Cohen, Billie Lee, Mike Maltese, Martha Goldman, John Burton, Harold Soldinger. *Seated on bench, left to right:* Betty Monahan, Dave Mitchell, Virginia Morgan, Ruth Pierce. © Warner Bros. Entertainment, Inc. Martha Goldman Sigall Collection.

"Sketch Pad Varieties" of 1939. Program and cast. © Warner Bros. Entertainment, Inc. Martha Goldman Sigall Collection.

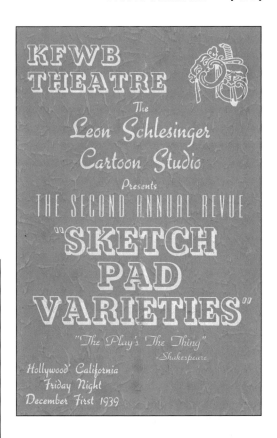

## "THAT'S MY CUE"
Words and music by Martha Goldman
Arranged by Milton Franklyn
Sung by Virginia Morgan

## "THE GIRLS"
By Mike Maltese

### CAST

Miss Forbes . . . Lois Waggoner
Mrs. Benznagle . . Gladys Hallberg
Miss Raye . . . . . Auril Blunt
Miss Wainright . . . Helen Sibert
Miss Haynes . . . Betty Monahan
Newcomer . . . Martha Goldman

Directed by Virginia Morgan

Scene:   A producer's office
Time:   Mid-afternoon

"Sketch Pad Varieties" of 1939. Inside page (6) showing name of the play, "The Girls." © Warner Bros. Entertainment, Inc. Martha Goldman Sigall Collection.

A little blurb in "The Exposure Sheet" read:

> Many Thanks—Thanks to all of you for your swell cooperation in helping us sell tickets for the "Sketch Pad." You might be interested to know that we will clear $40 which will go into our Christmas basket fund!

Gaining from their experience in 1938, this group decided that the money made from the prior year's show could be improved upon in 1939. The way we accomplished this was to make up a formal type of playbill for which we sold advertising to local businesses. Not only did we have the money from the admissions, but additional funds were generated from the playbill. And, for its time and purpose, it was a real nice presentation. The playbill was red on its front and back pages with silver lettering, which read:

> KFWB THEATRE,
>  The Leon Schlesinger Cartoon Studio Presents
> THE SECOND ANNUAL REVUE "SKETCH PAD VARIETIES," Hollywood, California,
> Tuesday Night, December First, 1939.

The first sketch was entitled, "Put Him On, Please," written by Henry Binder. Its cast was as follows:

> First Secretary..............Ada Ruinello
> Second Secretary.............Virginia Morgan

Sketch #2 was "Ours Not to Reason Why," written and directed by David Mitchell, and starring the following cast:

> Mrs. Brown..................Dixie Mankameyer
> Salesman....................Mike Maltese

A fifteen-minute intermission followed with Coca-Cola served outside. After intermission, a song that I wrote, "That's My Cue," was sung by Virginia Morgan. I originally wrote the song for one of the sketches that was going to be used. But about two weeks before the show, the main female lead left the studio, and we couldn't get anyone on such short notice to fill in for her. The sketch was dropped. Virginia thought so much of the song that she suggested keeping it in the show.

I actually "wrote" the song a couple of months earlier while taking a shower. As I stepped out of the shower, the song was almost complete. On Monday, when I arrived at the studio, I sang this song to Virginia, who suggested that I sing it to Jean Blanchard, who was a musician and who could write it in note form on a sheet of music.

Virginia sang my song to Mr. Schlesinger, who liked it enough to send it to the Warner Bros. lot with the suggestion that the studio orchestra record it. Milton Franklin made the orchestration for the twenty-seven-piece orchestra conducted by Leo Forbstein. They made a 33-⅓ speed record of it.

After the intermission, the recording was played off-stage, and Virginia Morgan came out to center stage and sang to the music. By their applause, the audience seemed to like the song, and quite a few people commented very favorably about it to me.

Sketch #3, "The Girls," was written by Mike Maltese and directed by Virginia Morgan. Shown at the top of the page on which this sketch appears is the name of the featured song: "That's My Cue, words and music by Martha Goldman."

The cast:

Miss Forbes.....................Lois Waggoner

Mrs. Benznagle.................Gladys Hallberg

Miss Raye.......................Auril Blunt

Miss Wainright.................Helen Sibert

Miss Haynes....................Betty Monahan

Newcomer.......................Martha Goldman

When we are working at the Warner Bros. Museum, my husband tells this story over and over again to the museum visitors. And I've asked him to do it here once more.

This is Sol, and this is how my story goes: I gather people around the display case in which this 1939 playbill is exhibited with the page opened to Sketch #3. I tell them how these shows in 1938 and 1939 came about and the reason for them. I explain what happened in 1938 and how, in 1939, they said to each other, "We have to do much better this year than we did last year, for there were so many people last year who needed our help and we weren't in a position to do anything for them because we didn't have enough money." So, they came up with the great idea of a much larger playbill in which they sold advertising, thus giving them not only the money from the twenty-five-cent admissions, but the money from the advertising as well.

On the opposite page, I point out to them that the song that was sung in the show that year was Martha Goldman's "That's My Cue" and that she also played the part of the Newcomer.

As I've told you, this playbill is from the year 1939. That, of course, is sixty-two years ago. We have a treat for you. Martha Goldman is with us today, for she is a docent at the museum and is working this afternoon." And, I proceed to point her out to my listeners. After many "oh's and ah's," I then inform them that "during those sixty-two years, Martha's name, of course, changed when she got married." This is followed by a few seconds for a "pregnant pause," after which, I add, "To me." You wouldn't believe the responses I get. I have never failed to get a laugh. Most of the times, those laughs are so loud that Martha, in the front of the room, says to herself, "Sol just told THAT story again."

One afternoon, I told this story to a group of young high-school girls who were visiting from Texas. From them, I got the nicest compliment yet when they said, "You just made our whole day for us." I informed them that, with that remark, they had done the same for me.

There was one occasion when Martha and I had been booked to work the museum on a Tuesday. During the prior weekend, we received a call from our grandson, Dustin, who was 16 at the time and who lives in San Diego, asking if it would be o.k. for him to come up on the train to spend that week with us during his summer school vacation. He knew we would be going to San Diego the coming weekend for his birthday celebration and could take him home.

Dustin knew the story I tell to museum visitors, but spent much of his time listening to me tell that story over and over again during the afternoon. He loved to watch the people I spoke with, especially the responses I received at the conclusion. The person that thrilled him, and me, the most was a young woman, probably in her late twenties who had a young son, probably three or four years of age with her. As I finished my story, she broke into tears. She was actually overcome with emotion for a few seconds and thanked me over and over again for sharing that story with her. Dustin, of course, told the story for several months to everyone who would listen, the story of how Grandpa made a woman cry.

With Martha usually at the front of the room and me at the rear, many of the people who have heard my story will stop Martha as they are leaving and make some comment such as, "Your husband is sure proud of you" or "Your husband is a great publicity agent for you." One elderly man and woman stopped to speak with her and asked for her autograph.

Now, back to Martha, for these really are her stories.

The fourth sketch was entitled "Animators Courageous" and was written by Chuck Jones and directed by Virginia Morgan. Its cast:

First Animator...................Harold Soldinger
Second Animator.................Dave Monahan
Third Animator...................Sid Sutherland

Other Animators.................Fred Jones
        Robert Atkins
        Philip Monroe
        Rudolf Zingler
Jimmy............................James Conner
Newsboy..........................Paul Callier
Smoky............................Henry Garner

Paul Callier, who played the "Newsboy," really was our newsboy. After school each day, he would sell the *Los Angeles Herald Express* at the studio. We "drafted" him for the part.

Inside the back page were these acknowledgments:

Our Many Thanks To
Harry Maizlish, General Manger of KFWB, for the use of the theatre and for his generous support.

We Also Thank
Paul Covert of KFWB.
Warner Bros. Property and Transportation Departments.
The Sketch Pad Varieties' Production Staff:
Stage Manager....................John Burton
Assistants.......................Paul Marron

Kenneth Moore

Alexander Ignatiev

Constantine Lebedeff

Roy Laufenburger

Another way we had of raising money for the Christmas baskets was our Monday night screening of a second run feature that Warner Bros. would send over to us. The screening was in the KFWB theatre and we invited family, friends, neighbors, even strangers. We had a full theatre almost every week. Admission was canned goods or money in any denomination people wanted to leave.

Just before Christmas, some of the fellows and girls would stay after work to fill large boxes that originally held film cans with the food we had been able to buy, including sugar, flour, potatoes, rice, pasta, and, of course, canned goods. The day we made our distribution, we would add the ham or turkey supplied by Mr. Schlesinger.

I was told later by one couple that the food lasted until the end of February and that they didn't know what they would have done without it. They were so appreciative.

# SONGS

Sol mentioned one of my songs earlier: "That's My Cue." I don't know where I acquired the ability to write songs in my head. I never studied music. But somehow I was able to compose a song, words and music, and then sing it to someone who could write it in note form. These songs were sung at the employee shows we put on for our family and friends.

Sometime in 1939 or 1940, Mr. Schlesinger was planning to have a radio cartoon show with Mel Blanc doing all the voices. This, of course, was before television. Knowing that I wrote songs, he asked me to write the theme song for the show, and I presented him with "You're a Merrie Melodie and I'm a Looney Tune." He liked it very much and gave it to Lee Hathaway to make up the cover for the sheet

Music sheet. Leon Schlesinger asked the author to write a theme song for a cartoon radio show he had in mind. The result was "You're a Merry Melody and I'm a Looney Tune." Lee Hudson designed the cover. © Warner Bros. Entertainment, Inc. Martha Goldman Sigall Collection.

music that would be sold after the show aired and the song, hope-fully, had become a hit.

He told her to change the spelling of the title to "You're a Merry Melody and I'm a Looney Tune" so as not to conflict with the spelling used in his copyrighted cartoon titles. He told me, "The song, of course, is yours."

The cover shows Bugs Bunny putting up pictures of Porky Pig and Petunia and a picture frame which reads, "Music and Lyrics by Martha Goldman." Bugs is hammering the last nail of a picture of Leon Schlesinger with the words "Leon Schlesinger, Producer of Merrie Melodies and Looney Tunes Animated Cartoons" beside it.

Leon was deeply into contract negotiations with KFWB for the Sunday night 8 to 8:30 slot when Maxwell House Coffee, a big radio sponsor in those days, came along and wanted two hours, from 8 to 10 P.M., for a variety show. KFWB was in the position of having to go with Maxwell House. They offered Schlesinger the 10:00 to 10:30 spot, but he told them that wasn't any good for all the kids would already be in bed since they had school the next day.

However, he liked the song so much that he sent it to Schirmer's Music Publishing in New York. They told him that, while it may have been a great theme for a cartoon radio show, without such a show, it had no commercial value. That was the end of my song, in that nothing ever came of it. But my romantic husband still loves it. And, our friend Jerry Beck, upon hearing it for the first time, exclaimed, "That song has got to be sung at my wedding."

Is eleven years later soon enough? Lucky for me, I didn't have to hold my breath, for it took Jerry eleven years to meet the love of his life, Marea Boylan. They were married on June 15, 2003, in the home of their friend Brad Kay. I did sing the "Merry Melody" song with the help of the host who is also a professional musician.

Several days prior to the wedding, I met with Brad at his home to rehearse. I brought the only sheet music I had and it proved to be inadequate. It was lacking in meters and had no chords. He patiently worked with me. I sang a few notes and he would write it on a sheet of music, correcting it as he went along. It took almost all afternoon, but when it was finished, it really sounded great.

After the wedding ceremony itself, with fifty or sixty guests attending, I did sing the song to a very receptive crowd. They really liked it. Other guests also sang, including the bride, who sang a number of songs. Brad accompanied all of us.

Later, a whole new group of people arrived who had been invited just for the reception and I was asked to sing my song again. They were another very receptive crowd, perhaps because so many of Jerry and Marea's friends in attendance were people from animation.

# [ *chapter 12* ]

# STRIKES

Working in the industry wasn't all fun and games. Most of us felt that we were underpaid. After a whole year at Schlesinger's, my salary was twenty-one dollars a week. At this point, I was called into the office and told that I was now a journeyman and that was the top salary they gave painters. I worked three years at that wage. Of course, I wasn't the only one. Everyone in all the departments felt they were underpaid, so the Schlesinger employees joined the Screen Cartoon Guild.

Our unit had months of fruitless negotiations with Mr. Schlesinger, and the Guild called a strike. Before we could put up a picket line, Schlesinger locked us out. The lockout lasted only a few days, after which we all received a special delivery letter asking us to report back to work. This we did, as he agreed to all the terms of the new contract. I was to get a five-dollar increase, and everyone else got raises accordingly.

But the family atmosphere that we had enjoyed for so many years began to change: the almighty buck had started to raise its ugly head.

On June 1 of that same year, 1941, the Disney people called a strike. All members of the Guild supported them, and wherever a Dis-

Strike notice, 1941. Letter from Leon Schlesinger to all the employees. © Warner Bros. Entertainment, Inc. Warner Bros. Corporate Archives. Chuck Jones Collection.

## Leon Schlesinger Productions
### 1351 N. Van Ness, Hollywood, California

May 17, 1941

TO THE EMPLOYEES OF LEON SCHLESINGER
PRODUCTIONS:

This day a communication was received from Mr. George E. Bodle, attorney for the Screen Cartoonists Local Union No.852, enclosing a proposed agreement between the union and Leon Schlesinger Productions and advising that unless the contract as proposed is accepted on or before Monday, May 19, 1941 at 10:00 A.M., same would be withdrawn. Mr. Bodle and your Mr. Charles M. Jones verbally informed us that unless the contract was accepted a strike would be called on Monday, May 19, 1941 at 10:00 A.M.

The terms are not acceptable and have been rejected and as a result we assume that a strike will ensue.

Enclosed herewith please find check in payment for services due to date.

Very truly yours,

Schlesinger lockout photo, 1941. *Left to right:* Ben Washam, Roy Laufenberger, unknown, Sue Dalton, Paul Marron, Martha Goldman. Photo by Chuck Jones. Courtesy of Chuck Jones Enterprises.

ney film was showing, people were assigned to picket. The entrance to the Disney studio was also filled with pickets.

Across the street from the Disney Studio, on the property now occupied by St. Joseph's Hospital, we set up a soup kitchen, and all of us contributed food and time for the strikers.

One day, we were told to dress in French Revolutionary costumes, and a lot of us showed up to picket in those outfits. We sure looked like members of the French Revolution. We were dirty and grimy with make-up, and we sang the following words to the tune of "The Marseillaise," France's national anthem:

> Come on, you faithful sons of liberty,
> We're here to give you moral aid.
> We will put the ax to Gunther Lessing,
> And the mess of boners he's made.
> Come on, gang,
> And, don't lose your nerve.
> And, we'll all be working tomorrow.
> We have no use for the scabs,
> They'll soon find out to their great sorrow,
> They'll have no friends left
> To beg or borrow.
> Come on, you're doing swell,
> The scabs can go to hell.
> March on, march on,
> There's sure to be
> A final victory.

Gunther Lessing was the attorney for the Walt Disney Studio.

One night, I was assigned to picket the Pantages Theatre in Hollywood which was showing Disney's *Reluctant Dragon*. There must have been at least thirty people picketing. The theatre had a uniformed doorman and, when anyone arrived by auto, he would run to open the car doors and greet them. Our purpose was to try to keep all of these people from going into the theatre.

That evening, a chauffeured limousine pulled up and the door-man rushed to greet them. A couple dressed formally, she with a long formal dress and he in full dress with a top hat, got out of the car. The chauffeur got out and handed the gentleman and the lady a picket sign, and they then joined us! It was Steve and Audrey Bususto-tow. Steve was one of the Disney strikers. It wasn't until 1998 that I found out the chauffeur that night was also another striker, Maurice Noble, who went on to become one of the foremost layout men in the business.

The strike lasted about ten weeks. Members of the Teamsters Union supported us by refusing to cross the picket line at Disney. Under pressure from many sides, Disney finally consented to binding arbitration. The ruling was in favor of the union. However, one of the provisions addressed the issue of rehiring people who had partici-pated in the strike. The agreement on this provision was relative to the rehiring of the strikers. Disney agreed to do so for a period of only ninety days, and at the end of that time, Disney terminated the employment of many of them.

# [ *chapter 13* ]

# WORLD WAR II

By September 1939, the European countries of England, France, and, later, the Soviet Union were deeply involved in a war with Hitler's Germany and Mussolini's Italy. Japan and Spain were sympathizers for the German-Italy (the Axis) cause. The United States was supporting England and France with supplies. Many people felt or believed, however, that our actual involvement of sending troops to join the fight was only a matter of time. It was still a shock when our country was attacked at Pearl Harbor, Hawaii, by Japan on December 7, 1941.

The following day, President Roosevelt planned to address Congress, and his speech was to be broadcast nationwide. This was so important that Mr. Schlesinger arranged for a radio to be hooked up to a loud-speaker in each department. We heard the president so eloquently refer to the Japanese bombing as "the day that will live in infamy," and ask Congress to declare war on the Axis countries. It wasn't long after that many of the fellows began to leave for war service. The studio had to hire many more people, not only for replacements, but also because they took on the additional work of creating the "Snafu" training films for the armed services. We had to get security clearance to work on those pictures. The FBI even went to our

Drawing by Chuck Jones of SNAFU and Technical Fairy First Class © Warner Bros. Entertainment, Inc. Warner Bros. Corporate Archives. Chuck Jones Collection.

neighbors to determine whether or not we were loyal American citizens. As a matter of fact, one girl never did get clearance, as her husband was found to be a member of the German-American Nazi Bund, and she had to be terminated. Questionnaires had to be completed, fingerprints taken, and identification badges had to be worn by everyone at work.

The government classified all these training films as "Top Secret." We in the ink and paint department were given only ten cels at a time so that we wouldn't learn the content of the pictures. If there was any wordage in the film, the supervisor had to do the inking and painting so that the girls wouldn't even see it.

In recent years, I have rented copies of these "Snafu's" to see what all the fuss had been and I can't, for the life of me, see what secrets they could have contained. Telling our service men to be careful of what they said to strangers, telling them to use mosquito netting over their bunks when in the field, and so forth. What was the big secret?

A number of men from all the studios, including ours, went into the service, and most of them were assigned to the first motion picture unit located at "Fort Roach" in Culver City, California. It was actually the Hal Roach studios. Some others were sent to Fort Monmouth, New Jersey, to be members of the Signal Corps, which was doing animation of some sort for the armed forces. Some of our men who went into the services had nothing to do with animation. Dave Brown, an assistant animator at Schlesinger's, who was a flyer in the U.S. Air Force, was the only colleague I knew who was killed when his plane was shot down. When the news got to us, we were all very saddened. Not only was he a good artist, but was a real nice guy besides.

Whenever one of our men from Schlesinger's left for the service, he was always given a watch, courtesy of the Looney Tune Club.

During the war, the actress Bette Davis started the Hollywood Canteen, a place where servicemen could relax, meet some of the movie stars, eat, drink, and be entertained during their off hours. Almost all the studio workers, including stars and executives, volunteered to work there.

I worked every Friday night, either dancing with the fellows, serving, working in the kitchen, or wherever else I was needed. There was always a show for the servicemen. Dinah Shore would sing, Groucho Marx would entertain in his fashion. It seemed, too, that every Friday night, Marlene Dietrich was there belting out a few songs and always ending with "See What the Boys in the Back Room Will Have." It was really something to see a glamorous movie star, after her performance, with an apron around her waist, telling us what to do in the kitchen. She was very organized, and it wasn't unusual to see her wiping off the tables or mopping the floors after everyone had left.

To me and many others, one of the worst aspects of the war was the removal of the Japanese people living in California, Oregon, and

Washington to internment camps. This was taking place so hurriedly that those people had very little time to get rid of their homes or possessions, and all of their remaining assets were frozen.

Most everyone I knew thought this was outrageously unfair. I thought about all my fellow students with whom I went to school who were Japanese. Even though I thought nothing could be done about it, I wrote to my California senators and congressmen to protest this action. The replies I received stated that it was done for their own protection.

I was under the impression that this was happening all over the country. I learned that it had only taken place on the West Coast. It didn't even take place in Hawaii where the horrible attack occurred. The military there did detain some individuals who were suspected of being spies, but the majority of Japanese residents were not even questioned.

Here in the United States, people were not faced with the serious hardships as they were in Europe. We didn't have to worry about daily air raids and their devastation. We were mostly concerned with food and gas rationing.

My father signed up to be an air-raid warden. Every evening, he would check to see that all the neighbors on our block had their drapes closed so that no interior light showed.

Most people volunteered their services to the Red Cross and other charitable organizations. Women knitted sweaters for our servicemen. People became more caring, inviting servicemen for holiday dinners, or giving them rides in their cars.

We cartoonists volunteered our time after work to produce animated cartoons that were made to boost morale. Cartoons such as "Any Bonds Today?" were made to encourage investments in government war bonds. This picture was shown in theatres all across the country and, at intermission time, the theatre lights would come up, and the ushers would pass a can asking for donations for the war effort.

In 1942, our family was faced with the devastating news that our beloved mother was seriously ill and, on March 13, 1943, she was gone from our lives but not from our hearts.

# [ *chapter 14* ]

# DEPARTING SCHLESINGER'S

By the middle of 1943, things had changed so materially at Schlesinger's that I told Mr. Schlesinger I was leaving. I had been offered a job at a smaller studio, Graphic Films. He was so angry that he refused to let me go. I told him that I had a chance to better myself and asked, "If you could better yourself, you'd do it, wouldn't you?" He said, "I would never do anything to hurt 'my kids.'" During the war, if one worked on anything connected to the war effort, you couldn't leave that job without permission. I had no choice, I reluctantly had to stay.

There was an inker in the studio who wanted Betty Brenon's job. Florence Hammontre "apple-polished" George Winkler, our supervisor, every chance she got, bad-mouthing Betty. The next thing we knew, Betty was out of a job. Several of us were upset about this, and I was quite outspoken about what had been going on. It just became unbearable to work under this person's supervision.

Sometime in October, Mr. Schlesinger left for New York to negotiate the sale of Schlesinger's to Warner Bros. Of course, we didn't know it then. Just before leaving, he spoke to me and said, "I'm going to donate a one-hundred-dollar war bond to a studio raffle to benefit Lucille Hazelton, whose husband is dying of cancer. Each day,

from 5:00 to 5:30, I want you to go around to the various departments and sell chances." Since I was still the president of the Looney
Tunes Club and I felt this was very generous of him, I was more than
willing to do it.

I explained the whole thing to George Winkler. I later wished
Leon had explained it to him, also. George gave me his permission
to do so. So the next day at five o'clock, I told George, "I'm going to
sell chances on the raffle now," and he answered, "Fine." When I
came back to my desk at 5:30 to gather my things to go home, he
blew up at me and said, "Where the heck have you been?" I was
shocked, but I explained to him that he had told me I could do this.
He said, "Oh, sure, sure, I forgot."

The next day, I went to him at five o'clock and told him I was
going to sell raffle tickets again. He even took five chances. When I
sold all the raffle tickets I could that day, I went back to my desk and
was, once again, confronted by George, who was even angrier this
time. I got angry, too, for this was getting to be unreal.

The third day, I again went to him at five o'clock and said,
"George, do I have your permission to finish selling the rest of these
raffle tickets or are you going to bawl the hell out of me when I come
back? I'm only doing what Mr. Schesinger told me to do." He said,
"Of course, Martha, don't mind me. I have so much on my mind. Go
ahead and take your time." By this time, everyone in the studio knew
what was going on.

I sold the rest of the raffle tickets and wondered what was going
to happen when I returned to my desk again. Most of the girls were
waiting and watching, too. Sure enough, he raised hell with me and
said he was going to send me to Ray Katz's office. I said, "George, I
think you're nuts, and when Mr. Schlesinger comes back from New
York, you're going to have to deal with him about this." He said,
"You go see Ray Katz right now." So I did.

Ray just blew up at me, too. He yelled and yelled. He never really
heard my explanation. He said, "What am I going to do with you?"
I thought about Graphic Films still wanting me and I said, "Why
don't you fire me?" He said, "That's a very good idea. Get your things
and get out." That's just what I did, but that was not the way I would

have chosen to leave Leon Schlesinger's. I think the incident with Betty Brenon was really the beginning of the end for me.

I wasn't home ten minutes when I got calls from Frank Tashlin, Chuck Jones, and Bob Clampett telling me they would get my job back for me, that they thought that what had happened was a very unfair thing. I told each of them that I really did want to quit, that I had a chance to go to work for another studio and would rather they did nothing. I also told each one how much I appreciated his concern. I had additional phone calls from many of my friends at the studio telling me how much they would miss me.

It wasn't long before Maxine Cameron, Werdna Benning, and Auril Thompson took me out to dinner and presented me with a scroll of background paper on which everyone in the studio signed his or her name. At the top, Maxine drew a picture of Bugs Bunny lowering the flag to half-staff and wrote the words, "Gee, Doc, Martha's gone. We feel awful." They also gave me many gifts that had been bought with money from a collection taken at the studio.

I was told that when Mr. Schlesinger came back and was told what had transpired, he was absolutely livid.

In 1944, Leon Schlesinger sold his animation studio to Warner Bros. Jack Warner installed Eddie Selzer as the producer. Eddie had no experience in animation, nor any sense of humor. An interesting story about him happened one day when the fellows in the story department were acting out gags for a new cartoon. Of course, there was a lot of hilarity going on and, as fate would have it, Mr. Selzer walked by at that moment. He stuck his head in the door and said, "What's all this laughter about? There's nothing funny about making animated cartoons!"

Another incident involving Selzer occurred when Mike Maltese and Chuck Jones were discussing a story line. Selzer stuck his head in their office and saw a poster of a bullfight. He remarked, "Don't ever make a picture about a bullfight; there's nothing funny about that." Immediately, Mike and Chuck started working on "Bully for Bugs," a bullfighting picture that turned out real funny. The public loved it.

One of Mr. Schlesinger's better qualities was that he hired capable people, relied on them, and didn't interfere with the work in the studio.

# [ *chapter 15* ]

# GRAPHIC FILMS,
# HERE I COME

The same night I departed Schlesinger's, I called Werdna Benning, who was the head of ink and paint at Graphic Films and told her my situation. She told me to report for work the next morning. They were located on Melrose Avenue near Western Avenue in Hollywood.

My first job was to check the finished painting of the girls who were doing this work at home freelancing. There was only one other person working in the studio besides Werdna, and that was Mary Sheridan, who painted the backgrounds. The boss was Les Novros, a former Disney animator.

We didn't stay in that location very long. The move took us to a little storefront on Beverly Boulevard near Doheny Drive. Here, Les hired more people, including David Hilberman and Gordon Ibsen. Dave was an animator and layout man; Gordon, a background painter. Soon after, Danny Miller was hired as a cameraman. Dixie Smith joined our ink and paint staff.

Les was a hands-on producer. He participated in every segment of the business. And he wanted us to learn the job of each other person in the studio. This was the biggest thing to me, for I learned the entire mechanics of animation. Even though I worked seven years at

Graphic Films. Once located at 666 N. Robertson Boulevard, West Hollywood, California. Martha Goldman Sigall Collection.

Graphic Films staff. *Top row, left to right:* Al Weiss, Larry Ravitz, Abe Liss, Jim Davis. *Third row:* Martha Kitchen, Mary Sheridan, Werdna Benning, Felix Zelinka. *Second row:* Ted Parmelee, Sterling Leach. *Front row:* Mildred ("Dixie") Smith, Gordon Ibsen, Martha Goldman, Barbara Begg. Photo by Felix Zelinka, 1945. Martha Goldman Sigall Collection.

Leon Schlesinger's and I knew there were various departments there, the only things I had learned were painting and inking and how to read an exposure sheet. I really got an education with Les.

I can relate a funny story that involved Werdna and Dave Hilberman. These two were always discussing politics. She tired of it after a while and asked him to quit bringing it up. He didn't listen. I suggested that she use a Yiddish expression and I proceeded to teach her how to say "Hock mir nisht kine chinik," which, in essence, means "Stop bothering me." The literal translation, though, was "Chop me not a tea pot." I'm sure you agree that it loses something in the translation.

Since Werdna was not Jewish, learning that Yiddish expression wasn't easy for her, and it took a lot of rehearsing. Finally, we thought she had it down pat. One day, Dave started up again and she thought, "Here is my chance." But she got confused and blurted out in English, "Oh, Dave, chop me not a tea pottle." When Dave heard this, he literally rolled on the floor and couldn't stop laughing for he realized what she was trying to say. I don't think he bothered her again from that day on.

Les connected with a man named Shirley Burden, who put up the money to finance Graphic Films. He had an office and staff on Robertson Boulevard who made live-action pictures. We needed more space and we took the upstairs, which was vacant. So we moved again.

The first thing we did was build desks, bookcases, and closets. The fellows did most of the work, but the girls chipped in under their directions. All of us got along very well. We did some commercials, but then we landed a navy contract that covered more training films. More people were hired, and I was given the opportunity to be the camera assistant to Danny Miller.

In those days, women weren't allowed in the Cameramen's Union. Because it was wartime and we were doing work for the navy, the union decided to issue me a work permit. I was told that as soon as the war was over, I would have to forfeit that permit. As far as the union was concerned, I didn't have to pay an initiation fee or dues.

Working on the animation camera was assuredly the most interesting thing I had ever done. I enjoyed it very much. Actually, I enjoyed every moment of my time at Graphic Films, regardless of what I was doing.

While still employed there, I heard that volunteers were being sought to work on a political film, *Hell Bent for Election,* promoting President Franklin Delano Roosevelt and sponsored by the United Auto Workers. The actual work itself was being done at United Productions of America (UPA). I did this at night, as an unpaid volunteer. Les knew about this, but had no objections. It was while working on this film that I met Mary Cain, an ink and paint supervisor.

I worked at Graphic Films until the end of World War II. The day that Japan surrendered, our work stopped because there was no further need for training films. But, more important to me, a phone call was received by the studio notifying them that my Cameramen's work permit was revoked. The union sure hadn't wasted any time.

Les Novros had to regroup after all of us were terminated, but several years later he got involved with the making of pictures for IMAX theatres and became very successful.

My contact with Mary Cain at UPA paid off in that she hired me to work there on a temporary basis. I had told her that upon Sol's return from Guam, after the end of the war, we were to get married in Brooklyn, where Sol's family and many of my relatives lived. That marriage happened on April 7, 1946, exactly two years to the day from the day we had met.

Speaking of April 7, let's go back to 1944 and our meeting. This has very little to do with animation, if anything. Lion 6, the code name for the group Sol was attached to in the navy, had been transferred to the former Tanforan Race Track in San Bruno, not far from San Francisco. The outfit had previously been located in Norfolk, Virginia, and everyone was given leave to go home and told that upon their return, there would be no further leaves given, as they would soon be going somewhere overseas.

On his very first day of work at Tanforan, which was on a Monday, Sol was on his way to the building where he would be working for the commanding officer. Coming out of the personnel office, who does Sol spot but his good friend Al Rapp. He knew Al did not work in personnel and asked what he was doing there. Al replied that he had family in Los Angeles that he hadn't seen in twelve years and had just been given a four-day pass for the coming weekend to visit them. Perhaps he had been able to wangle it because Passover and Easter were coming up.

Al was the type of person who could talk himself into or out of any situation. When he asked Sol to go with him to Los Angeles, Sol said, "Get me the pass and I'll go with you." Al turned around, went back into personnel, and came out within minutes with a pass for Sol, too.

It wasn't until Wednesday evening that they were able to go to the train station in San Francisco to make reservations for the trip. Upon entering the station, all they could see was a mass of people, all of them waiting in line to get tickets to somewhere. There was nothing they could do but get into one of those lines. After what seemed like an eternity, they found themselves at the ticket counter.

They asked the clerk for two round-trip tickets to Los Angeles. The clerk laughed out loud and said, "If anybody should know, you guys should know there is a war going on. You have to make reservations at least a month in advance." They explained that they had just gotten the passes on Monday and would soon be shipping out. The clerk became empathetic and said, "Let me see if there is anything I can do." With that, he walked to the back wall, where there was a shelf with telephones. He picked up the receiver of one and dialed a number. All the while he was talking, he kept looking up at a clock on the wall just above his head. About ten minutes later, he returned to Al and Sol and said, "You guys are lucky. I have two one-way tickets to Los Angeles that are supposed to be picked up by 8:15. It is now 8 o'clock and they haven't been picked up yet. I'm going to give them to you. But how you get back to San Francisco is your problem when you get to L.A." The fellows weren't worried, yet, about the good possibility of their being AWOL.

Al's family was just part of the eighteen people who attended that Passover Seder. Unfortunately, my mother had died a year earlier. But my father, my brother, and I had been invited to join several families who had known each other ever since we all lived in Rochester, New York.

I must tell you that there was another young girl there that evening who was literally throwing herself at Sol. As he tried to walk past her to take a seat at the far end of the table, she grabbed him by his navy shirt and said, "Sailor, you sit next to me."

I seated myself on the other side of the table at one end. When our friend Bea came into the room and noticed how we were arranged, she came over to me and said, "Martha, you can't sit here because I have to sit near the kitchen. But I have the perfect seat for you." She seated me right across the table from Sol.

After we all finished dinner, I was in the kitchen helping out with the dishes. Again, Bea approached me and said, "Martha, all the young people are in the living room singing to someone playing the piano. Why don't you go out and join them?" My reply, "Bea, don't worry, I'm going to marry that sailor one day!" On April 7, 2004, we celebrated our fifty-eighth anniversary. Parenthetically, Sol and Al did make it back to San Francisco on time.

To retrogress a bit, at the time I joined Graphic Films, the war was not going well for the Allied Nations in Europe. However, our troops in the Pacific were beginning to make progress by taking back some islands that were captured by the Japanese after Pearl Harbor.

Ted Parmelee, a director on our staff, brought a map of the world into the studio along with colored pins. We followed the daily progress the Allies were making on all fronts by moving the pins. The most epic aspect of the war happened June 6, 1944, thereafter referred to as "D-Day." On that day, our troops invaded Normandy, France, in an effort to recapture that country from the Nazis. This offensive resulted in tremendous casualties, but it signaled the beginning of the end for the Axis Powers.

At the studio, we were working on naval training films of a technical nature. But cartoonists will be cartoonists, and every day, the fellows sketched funny drawings lampooning the enemy. I retrieved and saved some of them to this day.

My brother Allan enlisted in the U.S. Navy and became a signalman.

Cartoon gags drawn by Ted Parmelee while on staff at Graphic Films. Martha Goldman Sigall Collection.

Cartoon by Ted Parmelee.

Cartoon by Ted Parmelee.

Cartoon by Ted Parmelee.

Cartoon by Ted Parmelee.

Cartoon by Ted Parmelee.

Sol and his outfit, Lion 6, left in a westerly direction to set up the Naval Supply Depot on Guam, although they didn't know that until arriving there. Their purpose was to supply the ships in what was then called the "Forward Area." The actual construction of the depot was done by naval seabees.

On November 7, 1944, Franklin Roosevelt was reelected for an unprecedented fourth term as president. Harry S. Truman became his vice president.

By early 1945, the tide of the war took a turn for the better on all fronts as the Allied Forces made extraordinary progress. The end of the war loomed closer.

On April 12, 1945, a very sad event took place. As FDR was taking treatments for a post-polio condition in Warm Springs, Georgia, he suffered a stroke and died. Truman was sworn in as president.

Our troops in the Pacific continued their assault on the islands held by the Japanese. Tokyo was bombed daily, but the Japanese refused surrender.

In the belief that the war would be shortened, on August 6, our planes unleashed an atomic bomb on Hiroshima. The devastation to lives and property was tremendous, beyond belief. This was the first time an atomic bomb was used. Still, no surrender was forthcoming. As a result, on August 9, an even more powerful atomic bomb was dropped on Nagasaki. This did bring a Japanese surrender on August 14, 1945. This became known as V-J Day (Victory over Japan).

The actual surrender agreement was signed on the battleship USS *Missouri* in Tokyo Bay, September 2, 1945.

On a recent trip to Hawaii, we actually stood on the deck of the *Missouri* on the exact spot that the surrender agreement was signed, a very moving experience. Interestingly enough, there is a copy of that surrender document in Japanese and another in English displayed there. The *Missouri* is now anchored in Pearl Harbor and open for tours.

# [ *chapter 16* ]

# MGM CARTOONS

After being married in Brooklyn, New York, Sol and I returned to California, for Sol had been accepted at UCLA under the G.I. Bill of Rights, and I was ready to return to animation. MGM was the closest animation studio to where we lived in Venice, at the beach, so I put in my application there. My first boss, back at Schlesinger's, had been Art Goble, who was now in charge of the ink and paint department at MGM, and he was the one who hired me on June 22, 1946.

The MGM cartoon studio was on lot 2, across the street from the main lot at Overland Avenue and Montana, a street that no longer exists. The building is no longer there either. It was torn down along with the outdoor sets that comprised lot 2. In its place are lovely homes and, on the spot where the cartoon studio stood, is senior housing.

When I went to work there in 1946, the cartoon unit occupied a two-story building. Its appearance was clean, inside and out. The walls were plastered and painted a light color. At Schlesinger's, wallboard had been nailed on studs, and the nails could be seen.

At MGM, the floors were linoleum block tiles and always clean and polished. At Schlesinger's, the wood floors were porous. The upstairs creaked and shook whenever anyone walked across the room.

MGM Animation Studio, Culver City, California. © Turner Entertainment Co. Courtesy of Bob Casino.

Cartoon caricatures of MGM staff. *Front row, left to right:* Herman Cohen, Carlo Vinci, George Bannon, Joe Finck, Jerry, Tom, Scott Bradley. *Second row:* Ken Southworth, Hal Elias, Bill Kirk, Bob Gentle, Jack Carr, Lovell Norman, Greg Watson, Ben Shenkman, Ken Muse, Irv Spence, Lew Marshall, O. B. Barkley. *Back row:* "Nate," Mike Lah, "Max" Maxwell, Dick Bickenbach, Frank Paiker, Joe Barbera, Bill Hanna, Ed Benedict, Lefty Callahan, Art Goble, Howard Hansen, Bill Schipek, Jack Nicholson (office boy, better known later as an actor). Drawn by Ben Shenkman. © Turner Entertainment Co.

At MGM, the desks and shelves in the ink and paint department were painted. At Schlesinger's, our desks were unfinished wood.

At MGM, the building was cleaned on a daily basis and the waste baskets emptied. At Schlesinger's, we were lucky if this happened once a week.

At MGM, the projection room had theatre-type seats. At Schlesinger's, we sat on wooden benches with no backs.

At MGM, I felt that I had gone from rags to riches. Nevertheless, what we lacked at Schlesinger's in ambiance could never be compared to all the fun we had there. I suppose my attitude was different also. I was married now, more mature, and involved in other things outside the studio.

The times were different, too. Our country had been in a World War for four years. We all grew up very fast. The entire atmosphere at MGM was more serious but by no means stuffy.

Everyone was friendly at MGM, and I made new friends, especially Colene and Frank Gonzales, Rita Giddings, Florence Heintz, Paula and Jim Faris, Jean Tobin, and many others. It was wonderful to be working for Art Goble again. Roberta Greutert was Art's assistant and very easy to work with. Some of my former friends from Schlesinger's were there, such as Suzie Williams, Irv Spence, Jack Carr, Bobo Cannon, Jack Stevens, Manny Corral, Tom Byrne, and Tex Avery. So it was like old home week for me. To make it more nostalgic, the first scene I was given to ink was from a picture directed by Tex entitled "Northwest Hounded Police."

There were only two units at MGM. The Tom and Jerry series was directed by Bill Hanna and Joe Barbera. Tex Avery's unit used a variety of characters and his famous "spot" gags.

Our production manager, C. G. Maxwell, was always addressed as "Max" and had the tremendous responsibility of making sure every cartoon was completed properly and in the prescribed time. So much planning and work went into the making of an animated cartoon.

Max was one of the first people hired in 1937 when MGM decided to operate its own cartoon studio located on the MGM property. He was hired as production manager and continued in that position until the studio closed its doors in 1957. It appears that MGM had quite a large backlog of cartoons for they were still releasing them through 1958.

Before Max came to MGM, he had more than ten years of experience. His career began with Walt Disney in Kansas City, and Max followed him to Los Angeles. He also worked a short time at the George Winkler Studio, then went with Harman-Ising during the time they directed the Looney Tunes and Merrie Melodies. When Harman-Ising left Schlesinger in 1933, Max left with them and stayed on until he was hired at MGM in 1937.

After a year at MGM as an inker, I was asked by Jack Stevens, the head cameraman, to be an assistant in the camera room. I had known Jack since I was a kid and he worked for Pacific Title. He and I also worked at Schlesinger's at the same time. I was overjoyed to be working with him and Manny Corral, the other cameraman. Manny was also at Schlesinger's when I started in the business. Any wonder why it was like old home week for me?

My duties included loading the cameras with raw film, keeping track of the amount of film used each day, getting the scenes ready for the camera, developing the daily pencil tests, setting up the publicity shots, and making matted setups of cels for the VIPs who came into the studio. One day, Hal Elias, our assistant producer, brought Katharine Hepburn through the studio. When he gave her one of the Tom and Jerry pictures I had matted, she insisted on meeting the one who had made that picture. So Hal brought her in to meet me. She took my hand and told me how talented I was. What a thrill to have such a famous and well-liked movie star take the time to thank me. It was completely unexpected for I had just been doing my job.

The camera department at MGM was very different from Schlesinger's. At MGM, the department was one large room with two cameras. The smaller one was used for pencil tests. The larger, newer camera was used for shooting the completed scenes. It also had a large table to enable the cameramen, when shooting, to have access to the scenes. At Schlesinger's, the work area was much smaller.

For those not familiar with "pencil tests," all the pencil drawings and paper background layouts of the cartoon were photographed to ensure that the action was smooth. By the time the drawings got into ink and paint and the paper layouts were rendered into backgrounds, the director could be confident the entire cartoon would be the way it was planned.

Located in the camera department was a very large open cabinet with cubbyholes into which were placed completed scenes of the picture ready to be shot. Of course, each scene was lined up in numerical sequence. At this time, the finished backgrounds were also brought into the camera room.

The cameramen, Jack Stevens and Manny Corral, alternated between the two cameras: the animation camera and the pencil test camera. Jack shot both the finished picture and the pencil tests for the Tom and Jerry unit. Manny did the same for the Tex Avery unit.

Prior to heading one of the MGM units, Bill Hanna had started with Harman-Ising when they were directing Looney Tunes and Merrie Melodies produced by Leon Schlesinger. When Harman-Ising broke with Schlesinger, Bill went with Harman-Ising, who were on their own for a while. It was in 1937 that Bill and a few others left Harman-Ising and were hired by MGM. A couple of years later, Hugh Harman and Rudy Ising were hired by MGM as directors.

This story of how Bill Hanna got into the business comes directly from Jack Stevens, who was married to Bill's sister, Marian. At the time, Jack was working at Pacific Title for Leon Schlesinger. Bill had a degree in engineering and had just finished working on the construction of the Pantages Theatre in Hollywood. These were depression days, and Bill was unable to get another job in his field.

He asked Jack if he knew of any jobs that might be available, and Jack suggested he go to the Harman-Ising studio, and that perhaps they could find something for him. That's exactly what he did, and they hired him as a cel washer! But before long, he was ink and paint supervisor and also contributing gags for the cartoons.

Joe Barbera worked at Van Beuren Associates in New York briefly. He then went to Terrytoons also in New York. After a few months, in 1937, he, Paul Sommer, George Gordon, and others were offered positions at MGM by Fred Quimby, head of the MGM cartoon studio in Culver City, California.

Within three years, they were offered the opportunity to jointly direct a picture entitled "Puss Gets the Boot." This cartoon became a very big hit. The cat is named "Jasper." The mouse doesn't even have a name. Even though Bill and Joe directed this picture, they weren't given screen credit. It was given to Rudy Ising.

Their next Tom and Jerry picture together didn't come for another year. It was in this picture that the characters' names were changed to Tom and Jerry. The name of that cartoon was "The Midnight Snack." It was this second picture, and the way it was received by the public, that put Bill and Joe into the spotlight, a light that has never dimmed.

Hanna and Barbera continued with the Tom and Jerry series for the next fifteen years, and during that period they earned seven Oscars for best animated cartoon:

    1943—"Yankee Doodle Mouse"
    1944—"Mouse Trouble"
    1945—"Quiet, Please!"
    1946—"The Cat Concerto"
    1948—"The Little Orphan"
    1951—"The Two Mouseketeers"
    1952—"Johann Mouse"

My favorite is "The Cat Concerto." This cartoon has a very smart look to it. In it, Tom is a very snobbish concert pianist who comes out onto the stage dressed to kill in white tie and tails. He puts on all the airs of a long-haired musician and proceeds to play Liszt's "Hungarian Rhapsody #2." All goes well until Jerry, who had been sleeping inside the piano, is awakened by the music. He rises and is shown to also be dressed in white tie and tails and comes out and plays on a tiny piano next to the grand. His selection, "On the Atchison, Topeka, and the Santa Fe," horrifies Tom. It was a very funny and clever cartoon.

I was able to enjoy it even as I was getting each scene ready for the camera. I just knew it would be a great cartoon. When it was screened for us, there were lots of laughs and much applause. We knew it was a gem.

Scene from "The Little Orphan." Directed by William Hanna and Joseph Barbera; animation by Irven Spence, Kenneth Muse, Ed Barge, Ray Patterson; musical direction by Scott Bradley, editing by James Faris. Academy Award winner, 1948. © Turner Entertainment Co. Courtesy of Bob Casino.

As directors, Bill Hanna, Joe Barbera, and Tex Avery made tremendous contributions to the success of their cartoons. They were fortunate, however, to have so many talented people who helped get these classic cartoons on the screen. The Hanna-Barbera animators were Irven Spence, Kenneth Muse, Ray Patterson, and Ed Barge. The assistants to these animators were Irving Levine, Barney Posner, Lew Marshall, Tom Byrne, and Lefty Callahan.

Richard Bickenbach was their layout man for many years. Bob Gentle painted the backgrounds. Vonnie Adamson Shaffer did the color models. Her job was to paint samples of all the animated characters and inanimate objects to determine the correct color to be used based on their appearance on the background.

Irene ("Pee Wee") Wyman was animation checker. Her job was to check every drawing in every scene to see how the animation and "camera moves" worked with the paper layouts. This was all done before every scene went to the camera department for pencil test.

The Hanna-Barbera unit remained constant during my time at MGM. But in Tex's unit, I remember many animators coming and going, including Ray Abrams, Robert Bentley, Preston Blair, Walter Clinton, Michael Lah, Ed Love, William Shull, Lou Schmidt, Grant Simmons, Gil Turner, Bob ("Bobo") Cannon, and Herman Cohen. The last three were my buddies from Schlesinger's.

The field of animation lost a wonderful man when Bill passed away on March 29, 2001. A memorial service was held the following Monday, April 2, at Warner Bros. Sol and I were among the hundreds in attendance.

## PRESTON BLAIR

Preston Blair designed the character Red Hot Riding Hood. This character caused quite a sensation. Preston, his wife, and baby lived across the street from where my family and I lived on Fernwood Avenue in Hollywood. Although I worked at Schlesinger's and he worked at MGM, we would always talk about the cartoon business and what was happening at each of the studios. He was a wonderfully talented animator and a great friend. I felt so bad when the state of California bought his home to make way for the Hollywood Freeway. I was happy to see him again when I was added to the MGM staff. After his leaving MGM, it was many years later, in 1985, that I saw him again upon his being honored by the Motion Picture Screen Cartoonists for his fifty years in animation. By the way, Preston got his start in animation at the Romer Grey studio, and he, like Ken Harris, had to pay Romer a weekly sum of money to be able to work in the studio to learn how to animate.

# IRVEN SPENCE

Irven Spence was considered an animator's animator. All the animators at MGM were extremely talented, but in my opinion and that of many others, Irv was just the greatest. He was a terrific person, but I also have to say he was "the biggest prankster" among many.

I think he may have caught the "prankster fever" when he was still at Schlesinger's, also known as the "Looney Bin." But Spence came up with the most intricate and well-thought-out pranks for his intended victims, especially Joe Barbera. Of course, Joe was no slouch himself and would retaliate, escalating the "feud." This went on time and time again.

It's no wonder Mr. Quimby walked down the halls muttering, "Those G——D—— high school kids." But he knew the work would get done and the cartoons would be very funny.

Irv started at Mintz and then moved on to Ub Iwerks. When Iwerks folded, Irv went to Leon Schlesinger's. I met him soon after I started there and quickly learned how talented he was.

When MGM built their own studio, he and other Schlesingerites went there. They were greeted by Mr. Quimby, who told them, "I know about the rowdyism that goes on at Schlesinger's and none of that will be tolerated at MGM." I could picture what was in their minds upon hearing those words. It was as if there were little balloons above their heads that said, "Oh, yeah?" Cartoonists will be gagsters. That's the nature of the beast.

Spence told me he really loved working at MGM and was hoping to spend the rest of his career there. When I was working as an inker, I could recognize Spence's scenes by the way the characters moved and by the expressions on their faces. Spence and I did not work together again, but we would meet periodically on various social occasions. I do know that he lost his only daughter and, soon after, his wife.

Anna Lois and Tom Ray lived just a few blocks from us in Culver City. Upon the occasion of their fiftieth wedding anniversary, many

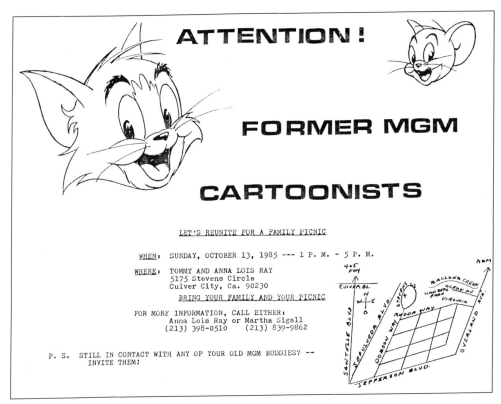

Notice of a 1985 MGM cartoon unit reunion at the home of Anna Lois and Tom Ray in Culver City, California. Elements under © of Turner Entertainment Co. Martha Goldman Sigall Collection.

people in the business attended. It seemed like a reunion of the entire cartoon business from the "golden age of animation." It was one of the most enjoyable events ever for all of us. You can't believe all the reminiscing that went on there.

Spence was there with his new lovely wife, "Ikie," whom I was so pleased to meet for the first time. As a sample of those in attendance, for I can't remember everyone, seated at our table were Maurice Noble and his wife, Marge; Norm McCabe and his wife, Fern; Lovell Norman and his wife, Estelle; and Peggi and Bob Matz. I also recall the presence of June Foray, Harry Love, and Gus Arriola and his wife, Frances.

In addition to his work at MGM, Gus was simultaneously producing his own comic strip, "Gordo," for the newspapers. It became one of the most highly acclaimed comic strips ever. For years, I had heard of this local boy who made good, but I had never had the opportunity to meet him. So I was delighted to talk with him and tell him what a fan I was of his work. He couldn't have been more gracious.

Art Leonardi and his wife, Shirley, were also there. Art and Tom go back to the late fifties at Warner Bros. when Art was Tom's assistant animator. Both men had very successful careers in animation, going on to be directors.

A few years later, Spence, who was suffering from Alzheimer's disease, and Ikie moved to Texas to be with her family. It seems that in no time at all, he was gone, at the age of eighty-five. Another great loss to everyone who knew and respected him and to the animation business as a whole.

## TEX AVERY—AT MGM

Tex Avery's tenure at the MGM cartoon unit began in 1942 and lasted until 1955. The first cartoon released under his direction was "The Blitz Wolf." Of course, as the title indicates, it had a World War II theme. This first effort has long since become a classic, as have many of his cartoons. Many of them are part of the Library of Congress Film Collection.

All of his cartoons were loaded with gags and each is carried to the extreme. In my opinion, Tex's style has been copied more than any other cartoon director.

It was Tex's good fortune to have these great animators in his first unit: Irven Spence, Preston Blair, Ed Love, and Ray Abrams. As some of these men left, they were replaced by equally excellent animators: Walter Clinton, Grant Simmons, Michael Lah, Robert Bentley, Louie Schmitt, William Shul, and Bob Cannon.

The only assistant animators I remember were Jim Escalante, Jack Carr, Bill Weber, and Ray Young. Tex had three storymen: Heck Allen; Rich Hogan, who came with Tex from Schlesinger's; and Jack Cosgriff. As was the case at Schlesinger's, you can be sure that Tex participated in every gag and every idea used in his cartoons.

He didn't have a regular layout man. He would draw a rough sketch of what he wanted. Mike Lah, Gene Hazelton, or Lou Schmidt would complete the layouts.

The only background man I remember was John Johnson, whom Tex brought with him from Schlesinger's. John painted the most beautiful backgrounds. Those long "pans" were especially beautiful and looked so realistic.

Marjorie Howe did Tex's color models, and when she left, Mary Lou Graham Manlove took over this position. Mary Lou started in the business as an inker at Harman-Ising, left with them when they left Schlesinger's, and went with them to MGM, where she remained until the studio closed.

Howard Hanson, another veteran from Harman-Ising days, was the animation checker for Tex's unit.

Al Grandmain and his assistant, Lovell Norman, animated the special effects for both units. Lovell had a great sense of humor and, it seemed, came into the camera room every day with a new joke. Al was a talented animator, but the most important things in his life were his wife and eight kids. He always talked about them, and I knew about every one of them. You can imagine how I felt twenty years later when I happened to meet one of Al's daughters, Jeannine, who was now married with her own children and who lives in our neighborhood in Culver City.

Through her, I met several other Grandmain "kids," and they really were as Al always had boasted. Jeannine's son Rick and our son Lee have been good friends ever since they were in elementary school. Rick and his family live here in Culver City, and he is the owner of a successful business, coincidentally, right next door to Cartoon Colour, a company that, for many years, supplied animation paint and materials to most of our cartoon studios in California and all over the world.

Sound effects and editing were done for both units by Jim Faris. Jim was well liked by everyone, and he married Paula Forbes, who was a final paint checker for many years. Jim began his career at MGM in 1946 as the assistant to the sound effects editor, Fred MacAlpin. Fred also headed the camera department. He didn't shoot the cartoons but had the responsibility to ensure that all of the camera equipment was properly maintained.

Fred also had the job of controlling the temperature of our building. Not only for the comfort of the employees, but the temperature had to be just right because of the way it affected paint and other equipment. There was a huge water heater at the back of the studio, and since we had steam heat, he needed to see that the temperature of the water heater remained constant. He also designed the layout of the studio before it was built.

I always felt that the studio was cool in the summer and comfortable in the winter. Of course, its location in Culver City may have had something to do with that. It is only six miles to the Pacific Ocean and is usually encompassed in the cool ocean breezes.

Fred MacAlpin was actually the first person hired by Fred Quimby when MGM decided to produce rather than contracting out their animated cartoons. He was promised that he would be head of the studio, which never happened. After working at the studio for over ten years, he was offered a much better job as a music mixer on the main lot. He recommended that Jim Faris be the one to take his place.

Jim told me that he was also to replace Fred as head of the camera department, but Jim suggested that the cameramen were capable of maintaining their own department.

Years later, Jim trained Lovell Norman to be his assistant until he, Jim, was offered a better job as editor for the *Ozzie and Harriet* television show. Lovell took over Jim's job until MGM cartoons closed its doors. Having had editing experience, Lovell became an editor in feature films on the main lot. Several years later, Lovell and his wife, Estelle, retired to Kingman, Arizona, and then, even later, moved to Florida to be near their children. Sadly, both of them passed away in the year 2000.

Scott Bradley handled the music for both units. And, like Carl Stalling at Warner Bros., Scott had access to MGM's musical library. He did all the music almost from the time MGM started its cartoon unit until the time it closed.

As in all the studios, the ink and paint department at MGM painted all the cels for every picture for every unit. Art Goble was our much-loved supervisor. His assistant, Roberta Ritchie Greutert, handed out the work. She, too, was very well liked and efficient in her work. I must say, she was the fastest woman walker I have ever encountered. If you were walking with her, you had to actually run to keep up. She was quite tall and able to make long strides.

As I've mentioned before, one of my duties in the camera room was to take the cels and backgrounds from the picture and put them together into setups. I would make seven or eight of these and have Hal Elias, our assistant producer, come in to approve them. He would take them to the publicity department on the main lot. They would be photographed and printed into 8" x 10" glossies, which would go along with each cartoon to the theatres and be exhibited as lobby cards.

After the cels and backgrounds were photographed, Hal would bring back the setups and, if they were suitable, I would mat them so they could be given out to the VIPs when they visited the studio. I never saw the glossies or gave much thought to them.

However, just a few years ago, Howard Prouty, archivist for the Library of the Academy of Motion Picture Arts and Sciences, was taking Sol and me on a tour of that library. It was fabulous to see all the memorabilia that has been collected about the motion picture business.

When we were almost finished, he asked me if there was anything special I would like to see. Of course, I asked if the library had anything on animation. He led us down to the basement, where there were rows and rows of cabinets, each labeled with the name of the cartoon studio as the source of the material it contained. The first one we came to was MGM, and he asked for the name of any cartoon and the year it was made. I immediately thought of "The Cat Concerto." He opened one of the drawers and brought out those 8" x 10" glossies. A wave of nostalgia came over me—glossies I had never

Scene from "The Cat That Hated People." Released in 1948 and re-released in 1956. Directed by Tex Avery; story by Heck Allen; animation by Walter Clinton, Louis Schmitt, William Shull, and Grant Simmons; music by Scott Bradley; editing by James Faris. © Turner Entertainment Co. Courtesy of Jerry Beck.

seen, glossies that had been made from the setups I had made fifty years before! What a thrill! It was so exciting to see, for the first time, the results of one of the things I used to do in the camera room.

Early in the 1940s, with the departure of Hugh Harman and Rudy Ising, the studio needed another director to head the unit, and Tex Avery made his appearance. He was allowed to develop his ideas, and the results were hilariously funny cartoons. It's hard for me to pick a favorite of his because there are so many, but "The Cat That Hated People" stands out in my mind.

This cat had every reason to hate people because he was so mistreated by everyone. He is so frustrated and disgusted that he wants to get away from it all. He sees an ad for a rocket ship and decides to go to the moon. He boards the ship, pushes a button, is propelled skyward, and ultimately, lands on the moon. He is momentarily thrilled, for the moon is the home of crazy creatures. But his joy is short-lived because every type of conceivable gadget attacks him unmercifully. Each one is out to destroy him. After being subjected to these horrific things, he is at his wit's end and decides the earth is not such a bad place after all. He pulls down a shade that becomes a golf course and, with a golf club in hand, he tees himself off and lands back on earth on a cement sidewalk. We next see him lying flat like a doormat while people walk all over him. He loves it, though, and has a look of contentment on his face as the cartoon ends.

It didn't take much to happen in the studio for someone to make a drawing illustrating the funny situation. I was the cause of one of them. I was on my way back to work from lunch. It was a rainy day, and I was stopped in my car at the corner of Overland and Montana, and waiting for a car coming in the opposite direction at a high rate of speed. Since this was before the day of directional signals, I had my window down and my hand extended despite the rain, signaling for a left turn.

Unfortunately, the fellow driving the car approaching me was not concentrating on his driving, but was engaged in conversation with a woman passenger. I learned later that he was on his way to the airport and was afraid of missing the woman's plane.

All of a sudden, he looked up and thought I was going to turn in front of him. He slammed on his brakes, skidded, clipped my left fender, then slammed into two cars parked at the curb, and moved them approximately ten feet even though they had their brakes set. You can just imagine how fast he was going.

Fortunately, no one was hurt, but when I got out of the car to examine the damage and to exchange information with him, I, nervously and unthinkingly, rolled up the window since it was still raining. Several of the people came out upon hearing the crash, among them Tex Avery. He noticed my rolling up the window, walked over to my car and rolled it back down. (How could I have been signaling for a left turn if my window was rolled up?) Good old Tex!

By the time I got back into the studio, on the bulletin board was a picture of Tex with the collar of his raincoat turned up, his hat pulled down over most of his face, and, surreptitiously, rolling down the window of my car. I don't know why I never took the picture home; it would have been a great memento for me.

When I started at MGM, I heard a story of an event that had happened before my time: one of the animators had a habit of putting his discards, or animation sheets on which he had made mistakes, on top of his desk and just letting them pile up instead of throwing them away. They were all from different scenes, all different productions.

One day, Mr. Quimby, the producer, came into one of the animator's room and noticed that stack of drawings. Since he had always seen animators flipping the scenes, he proceeded to do the same thing with these discards, of course, not knowing what they were. When he finished, he put them back on the desk and said, "This is going to be a very good picture." Remember Ray Katz flipping the music sheets at Schlesinger's?

I was working at MGM during the time that they were making the feature film *Singin' in the Rain*, with Gene Kelly. It was being shot on New York Street, which was adjacent to the cartoon unit. They had the set completely covered with tarps. Over and over and over again, we kept hearing the music for that rainy dance scene for what must have been every day for months. As beautiful as that song was, we sure did get more than tired of it. Everyone would groan every time it came on. "No, not again!" We had no idea what the name of the song was or what the picture was about. But all of us could have, and maybe did, hum that song in our dreams.

One of the good things about working at MGM was that we were able to eat in the commissary and see so many stars, Frank Sinatra, Clark Gable, Robert Taylor, Red Skelton, Fred Astaire, and Judy Garland. Judy's daughter Liza Minnelli was only two years old at the time she was brought into the commissary by a nanny who left her alone. She was seated by herself at a table for ten and as everyone passed by, she would look at them with her big brown eyes and ask, "Have you seen my daddy?" Shortly thereafter, nine men came in, including her daddy, the director Vincent Minnelli. With Daddy there, her face reflected happiness and contentment.

One day, during lunch, I wandered out on to the back lot and, standing about twenty feet in front of me, but with his back to me, was a tall man. I had no idea who he was. As though he could feel my eyes on him, he turned around and I immediately recognized him as Robert Taylor, the handsome movie actor. I have to admit my knees got weak. We smiled at each other—and that was it.

One day in the commissary, Red Skelton came in. He sat down at the first table with a vacancy and talked to the people already seated there. He would stay a few minutes and then move on to another table, from table to table to table. We thought, he sure knows a lot of people, when suddenly, he sat down at our table! He spoke with us like we were old friends and asked what we did at Metro. When we told him we were from the cartoon unit, he got so excited and asked a lot of questions about the cartoons produced in our unit. With the answers in his head, he moved on to another table. We were thrilled!

Every Monday, Wednesday, and Friday, cartoons and short subjects produced at other studios were shown to us during our lunch hour so that we could see what others were doing. Also, on our breaks, we always had a volleyball game going. Our star player was John Boersema, who was six feet four inches tall and had the great ability to spike the ball. Needless to say, everyone tried to get on his team.

## ANIMATION AND LIVE ACTION

In 1945, the MGM musical film *Anchors Aweigh* was being shown in wide distribution all over the country. It was very well done and lighthearted, the type of entertainment that was very much needed at that time in our nation's history.

Every musical number was of top-notch quality. However, one in particular was especially popular with the movie-going public. It was a scene that combined live action with animation. The musical sequence shows Gene Kelly doing a tap-dance routine with Jerry

Mouse. Gene and Jerry's dance steps were perfectly synchronized. The people seeing this segment cheered and cheered after it was over. I saw this movie at least five times, and it was received the same way with each audience.

I wasn't working at MGM in 1945, nor did I have any thoughts that I would be working there the following year. But, when I did join the cartoon department in 1946, *Anchors Aweigh* was still very fresh in my mind. Everyone who had been involved in the production was still very enthusiastic. One thing that surprised me was hearing that originally Gene Kelly had wanted to do the dance routine with Mickey Mouse. I thought the person who told me this was kidding. I found out differently. Gene Kelly really did want to dance with Mickey Mouse.

Many of the executives and movie stars apparently did not know that MGM possessed a cartoon studio and that we had our own mouse. I happened to be watching a video many years later called "When the Lion Roars," which included a number of MGM features.

Appearing in one of the segments was Stanley Donen, the musical director of *Anchors Aweigh*, who said he had the idea to combine live action with animation. He would have Gene Kelly dance with Mickey Mouse. Gene also liked the idea, and the two of them actually met with Walt Disney. When they presented their idea to him, Walt said, "Let me get this straight. You want Mickey Mouse to be in an MGM picture?" Gene and Stanley replied, "Yes." Walt answered, "Mickey Mouse will never be in an MGM picture." And that's how Jerry became Gene's partner in this sequence of the film.

Gene was filmed doing the entire dance routine. He was photographed against a blue backing. By this process, high contrast mattes are made that are both positive and negative of Kelly. The animation is shot with the matte in the camera holding back the exposure of Kelly. The negative is then backed up and the reverse matte is loaded into the camera and the negative of Kelly is exposed and the animation is holding back the light except for Kelly's figure. That combination camera work was done in our optical department at MGM. The film of Gene's dance steps was then rotoscoped and traced on to drawing paper. Using these drawings as a guide, Jerry was animated to match every movement. The next step was to ink, paint, and photograph all the cels.

At first glance, the rotoscope machine in our camera room looked like an animation drawing board. It had a round glass disk fitted with top and bottom pegs. The only noticeable difference was a small wheel with film sprockets that was attached to the lower left side of the board. Anyone operating this device could, by turning the wheel, advance the film one frame at a time. The film could be magnified and projected to the 10" x 12" size of animation paper. A mechanism inside the board made this process possible.

After the success of *Anchors Aweigh*, everyone on the main lot knew MGM had a cartoon studio. From that time on, many of the film production companies associated with MGM that were planning to use animation in their feature, came to us. They were generally small jobs, but in 1949, we had another interesting project.

We didn't know it at the time, but the name of the movie-to-be was *The Barkleys of Broadway*, with Fred Astaire and Ginger Rogers. Our involvement was in a musical number with Fred Astaire. He would not be dancing with any of our cartoon characters. In this number, Fred is the proprietor of a "theatrical shoe shop."

As the scene opens, we see customers bringing their shoes in for repair. One man needs his taps replaced and, after he leaves, Fred closes the door and pulls down the window shade, as the shop is now closed. He places the shoes on the counter and relaxes against it. Almost immediately, the shoes start to dance by themselves. This amazes him, and he gets the idea to put them on his own feet. They get his feet moving in a dance number that he seems to have no control over. The shoes dance, and his feet just follow.

Soon six other pair of shoes jump off the shelves on which they were placed and join in Fred's routine. How did they do that? By animation, of course.

Fred was filmed dancing in a pair of these shoes. When the film was processed, the tedious job fell to Lovell Norman, of our special effects department. After rotoscoping, Lovell would trace only the shoes, frame by frame, on to animation paper. He worked weeks in our camera room where the rotoscope machine was located.

MGM Christmas party, 1948. The poster was made specifically for this Christmas party. Mike Lah joins the author in completing the cutouts. © Turner Entertainment Co. Martha Sigall Goldman Collection.

Mike Lah, Mary Lou Johnson, Irene Wyman, and Alberta Lah. Mary Lou Johnson is pictured with friends after receiving the Golden Award from the Motion Picture Screen Cartoon Guild, Local 839, IATSE, June 6, 1987.

Irene Wyman, who was affectionately called "Pee Wee" because of her diminutive height, did the animation checking on this scene. It was her job to list on the exposure sheet the movements of the shoes, all six pair. The inkers, using a sliding celboard, traced the shoes on to the cels in their proper place.

The painters followed by painting each of the shoes white. They also had the added work of "backing up" the white of each shoe with a gray color so that each cel would be absolutely opaque. The reason they did this was that the animation was going to be combined with live action. The cameraman had to shoot each cel over lights underneath the camera.

My job during all of this was to get the scenes ready for the camera and to check whether all the cels were in the right order.

When Jack Stevens finished shooting the scenes, I took the film magazine into the darkroom and unloaded the film into a can to be sent to Technicolor. Now, it was the lab's job to perform its magic.

The very next day, the whole dance sequence was shown to us, and everyone was happy with the results.

Subsequently, our cartoon unit did other sequences for feature films such as *Dangerous When Wet*, with Esther Williams, and *An Invitation to the Dance*, again with Gene Kelly.

## MGM STUDIO ROMANCES

Colene Stultz married Frank Gonzales. Colene was an inker, and the best I've ever known. Colene started in the business at Disney, where she worked for about a year. This was followed by her work at MGM where she remained for many years. It was here that we got to know each other although our friendship deepened when we both worked at Celine Miles Ink and Paint.

Frank started in the business as an inbetweener. He became an assistant animator while he was at Warner Bros. (Remember how Speedy Gonzales got his name?) It was at Disney that he became a full-fledged animator. He finished his career at Filmation after becoming a layout man. Colene and Frank have retired to Dolan Springs, Arizona.

Paula Forbes married Jim Faris. They have retired in northern California.

Grace Enright married John Boersema. John started as an inbetweener and became an animator. Unfortunately, they divorced after seven or eight years of marriage.

Muriel Berger, a painter, was engaged to Greg Watson. They were together for the rest of their lives, but never married.

Shirley Ballou, an inker, married Bill Weber, assistant animator.

In 1949, Sol was graduated from UCLA, and we went back East to visit family. Upon our return to California, Sol went to work for an accounting firm and soon after became a CPA. Later that year, I left MGM, with the intention of starting a family. We had two boys, Bob and Lee, and after they were past the toddler stage, I started picking up work to do at home, working freelance. I worked for Celine Miles Ink and Paint for many years, Kurtz and Friends, C & D Ink and Paint, DePatie-Freleng, Film Fair, Bill Melendez, who did the Peanuts Gang, and Hanna-Barbera.

# [ *chapter 17* ]

# CELINE MILES
# INK AND PAINT

Celine Miles started in animation at Leon Schlesinger's in 1936. She was only there a year when she went to MGM.

Celine became head of ink and paint at Jerry Fairbanks while they were doing the series "Speaking of Animals." She next worked for Paul Fennell and then went into business for herself in 1954. I had heard that she had opened an ink and paint studio and, since I was looking for freelance work, I made my way to her studio in Hollywood. I was hired. I would pick up my work in the morning and work on it at home until it was finished. It was at this time that I had two young sons at home and was unable, therefore, to work in a studio.

The first thing that I worked on was a television series entitled *Q. T. Hush* for Lou Zukor, Rudy Cataldi, and John Boersema, the producers. We also worked on a series of commercials for Western Airlines and many other companies. We did lead-ins for television programs such as the cleaning woman introduction to the *Carol Burnett Show*. Also at this time, we did spots for the Jackson Five when they did a program named *Soul Train*.

When Michael Jackson was ten years old, he came into the studio with one of his older brothers, and he was fascinated with the work we were doing. He was such a darling, sweet boy. After he left, I remarked how nice he was, and Olaya Stevenson, another woman

Celine Miles studio. Celine's first ink and paint studio on De Longpre Avenue in Hollywood, California.

working at Celine's, said, "Martha, that was Michael Jackson from the Jackson Five." My reply was, "Who are they?" Everyone was astonished that I didn't know who they were and how famous they already had become. I guess I wasn't "with it."

We worked on a lot of television specials for Chuck Jones Productions, among them "A Connecticut Rabbit in King Arthur's Court" and "The Bugs Bunny/Road Runner" movie.

There were several specials for Warner Bros. We always helped Bill Melendez on his Peanuts Gang specials from the first one, "Charlie Brown's Christmas." We worked on Ralph Bakshi's "Fritz the Cat," the first cartoon, to my knowledge, to be X-rated. However, none of the scenes that we worked on at Celine Miles even came close to requiring such a rating. Those that did were done in the Bakshi studio. There was one woman at Celine's who refused to work on any of the Bakshi material.

We also handled animation for medical purposes and educational films. In addition, John Hubley would send a big package of work from New York every few months. We did quite a bit of work for him. The last picture we did was a special feature, "Doonesbury," based on the well-known comic strip.

We were invited to the screening of this picture and, as we arrived at the theatre, we learned the sad news that John Hubley had passed away. He was a brilliant animator.

In the mid-1970s, one very interesting job that we did was to help Murakami-Wolf finish a picture they were doing. Murakami-Wolf, an independent cartoon studio, was contracted to do the animation for a coming TV special, "Free to Be Me." This was co-produced by Marlo Thomas. She and many famous actors were involved in the live-action portion. This special was geared toward children and with the theme to make them feel good about themselves.

We did several scenes. The first one we did was tremendously long and quite complex, yet very enjoyable for us to work on. Celine told us that the live-action part of the scene takes place on a merry-go-round. Real child actors, including Michael Jackson, are riding and singing as the merry-go-round makes several complete rounds. Suddenly, the riders and the horses they are on leave the merry-go-round and gallop off into the countryside. That's the time they all become animated. The horses are beautifully drawn and painted like real merry-go-round horses. It took six of us over a week to do this particular scene. At the end of the special, the riders and horses come back and reenter the merry-go-round.

When we saw the finished picture on TV, we could see that the timing of the transition from live action to animation and then back again was flawless. The entire picture was upbeat and very enjoyable.

I was with Celine for about twenty-five years on an on-and-off basis. When the work came to a stop, I went elsewhere. When that work came to an end, I went back to Celine's, if she had work. Some of the people who also worked there were Colene Gonzales, Olaya Stevenson, Grace Boersema Jeffries, Vivian Byrne, Suzie Williams Dalton, Sylvia Brenner, Anna Lois Ray, Uvon Young, Paulino Garcia, Chandra Powers, Patty Richards, Stacy Maniskas, and a host of others.

Celine sold her busines in 1979, and she and her husband, Andrew Marcus, retired to Grass Valley, California. In 2003, they moved to Tucson, Arizona, to be near family.

# [ *chapter 18* ]

# WORLD EVENTS
# OF THE 1950S AND 1960S

The United States was barely recovered from World War II and was enjoying peace and prosperity when we became involved in a United Nations police action in North Korea. This war dragged on many years, with numerous casualties on both sides.

In 1960, John F. Kennedy was elected president of the United States. On November 22, 1963, while he and the First Lady were visiting Dallas, Texas, their motorcade was attacked and JFK was assassinated. The Texas governor, John Connelly, riding with them, was critically wounded, but recovered. The loss of our president was greatly felt by the country, the world, and especially his family.

Another loss to our country was the assassination of Martin Luther King Jr., a prominent leader of the black people of this country, on April 4, 1968. On June 6, 1968, Robert Kennedy, after claiming victory in the California Democratic primary election for president, was murdered in Los Angeles.

A technical advance in the field of animation during the 1960s was the invention by Ub Iwerks of a new machine that could xerox ink lines on to animation cels. This machine was capable of printing out many more cels in one day than could be done by any inker. I was told that this machine was able to turn out one thousand cels a day instead of the approximate fifty done by an inker. Inkers were forced, therefore, to go back to painting or other departments.

The ink and paint departments were also adversely affected when some studios started sending inking and painting to foreign countries such as South Korea, the Philippines, and Australia. In these countries, the pay scale was markedly lower than in the United States. The fact that the work sometimes was poorly done and had to be corrected after its return didn't seem to deter the studios. Would the animation itself follow? It sure did. The storyboard, the recording of the dialogue, and the instructions on the exposure sheets were still done here. But, all of the animation was sent overseas.

When computers were introduced here in the United States, the work initially returned here as well. However, the studios overseas soon became computer-oriented themselves and the work again started flowing to the foreign countries. I want to emphasize, however, that at no time was all the work being done elsewhere.

# chapter 19

# LISBERGER PRODUCTIONS

This company was originally an East Coast-based animation company that had a contract with NBC Television to make animated segments to be telecast during the 1980 Summer Olympics in Moscow, Russia.

Each segment would consist of an animated animal performing an Olympic event just prior to the showing of the actual event. All these segments would be combined into a full-length animated feature called "Animalympics." This feature could be shown in its entirety at movie theatres, on television, or on videotape after the completion of the games.

Steve Lisberger, a very talented young animator who was only twenty-seven at the time, not only produced, directed, and designed all the characters, but was an integral part of the writing team as well. There were upwards of thirty characters to be used, and each of them was highly stylized.

The picture had been started in the East, but soon Steve headed West and opened a small studio in Venice, California. The building he located in had at one time housed a grocery market. When empty, the building was like an open warehouse, but it wasn't large enough to hold all the people needed to complete the picture. Much of the work, then, was farmed out to freelance animation people, I among them.

My longtime friend, Auril Thompson, was head of the ink and paint department. She was an excellent choice, for she had the experience Steve needed. To start, she inked and painted all of the color models of each character. Then she hired some of the best inkers and painters she could find, Colene Gonzales, Raynelle Day, Peggi Matz, Nancy Thompson Katona (Auril's daughter), and Judy Cassels, among others.

Auril did all the special effects, which added so much to the beauty of the picture. She also did the final checking before each scene went to camera.

I did quite a few scenes, but the one that stands out in my mind was the one I did about two marathon runners who were competing against each other. One of the characters is a goat (French, yet) by the name of Rene Fromage, a self-assured and egotistical champion. His closest competitor is Kit Mombo, a sleek lioness from Africa. Bill Kroyer animated that scene.

As they run mile after mile through the beautiful countryside, their thoughts can be heard and seen in "balloons" above their heads. At first, their thoughts are critical of each other. As they keep going, they become more appreciative of each other. Their feelings progress to the point, as they finish the race, they are holding hands. Isn't this what the Olympic Games are all about? This scene seemed to take me forever, just like a real marathon.

Another reason I will not ever forget that scene happened something like this:

The metal desk on which I did my work held six moveable wooden shelves. One day, I had finished the scene, but the paint on the cels was still wet. In order to facilitate the drying process, I moved some of the shelves elsewhere in the room to expose the cels to more of the air. As I was carrying one of the shelves at eye level, I forgot that our son Bob, who was home from Hawaii, had left his suitcase on the floor of the room. I tripped, the board hit me on the nose, and the cels went flying.

The wet paint was red and when Sol came running, we couldn't tell if it was all paint or if there was blood mixed into it. He handed me a box of Kleenex, and I pressed some to my nose. One look told us there was blood. Finally, I was able to stop the blood and sat back down to repair the cels.

It wasn't until about two months later that I learned I had fractured my nose in two places. My doctor insisted that I have surgery to facilitate my breathing.

When the picture was finished, it was shown at a special screening at the Goldwyn Studio in West Hollywood for all who had any connection with it. It was extremely well received. The idea and the story were perfect for its purpose. The animation was well done. The backgrounds were beautiful, and the music added so much enjoyment to the picture. The voices were done by Gilda Radner, Billy Crystal, Michael Fremer, and Harry Shearer.

A gala wrap party had been scheduled, but when Sol and I arrived, we were told that something completely unforeseen had happened. President Carter had cancelled the United States participation in the Olympic Games because Soviet Russia had invaded Afghanistan. I could not believe what I was hearing and thought it was a bad joke. Many of us must have felt that way, but a joke it wasn't.

NBC cancelled its contract and, with it, months and months of work and millions upon millions of dollars from Lisberger and his investors went down the drain. Steve was already working on his next project when this bombshell exploded. It was to have been an animated science fiction picture entitled "Tron." Now there would be no financing for it. He eventually went to Disney with the idea and it was done there.

And what about "Animalympics"? It has been shown on television many times in recent years and can be purchased on videotape, but it couldn't possibly have the impact it would have had if the Olympic Games had gone on as scheduled.

# [ *chapter 20* ]

# KURTZ AND FRIENDS

As a freelance painter, I did a lot of networking. I always tried to find out which studio had a lot of work to offer. I heard about a fairly new studio named Kurtz and Friends. It was located on North Whitley Place, above Hollywood Boulevard. The studio occupied buildings that at one time were residential bungalows joined together. These types of buildings were called "courts."

I knew I would like working there, just by looking at its hokey logo, and once inside, I really knew I would like to work there. All the rooms were decorated artistically. Recently, I spoke with Bob Kurtz and asked for an explanation of his logo. He told me that it was a one-body, two-headed beast with the heads looking in opposite directions. The character is on stilts and the creature on its back is Bob himself. It sure doesn't look like him.

I applied to Jan Cornell, head of ink and paint, who hired me and gave me a whopper of a scene from a Chevron commercial. They used a style of inking that was different from anything I had been used to. They purposely used thick, wobbly lines. This was the style of Robert Peluce, who was the designer at Kurtz and Friends.

Raynelle Day, a friend from Schlesinger's and Snowball, was one of the inkers. She did a beautiful job of inking this very different style. Other inkers were Marsha Sinclair and Maria Alvarez. The painters were Betty Frederick, Edith Simpier, and Gyorgyi Peluce. Robert Peluce was art director, and Libby Simon was his assistant.

I was delighted to see Libby, who grew up in Culver City and was a schoolmate of our son Bob. I also knew her mother, Millie Simon, when she was a painter and later became a partner in Simba Enterprises, an ink and paint service.

You would expect the characters to be animated, but everything, except a colored sky card, was animated. The backgrounds were animated. If the background was a hill, a gas station, or a rock formation, it all moved—and in a big way! Some of these commercials were thirty or sixty seconds in length, but it took weeks to complete each of them. The results, however, were awesome. I wish Chevron would issue them again so that a new generation could see what we did. Bob Kurtz won many awards for these spots.

Kurtz and Friends did commercials for other companies as well. One I remember vividly because I worked on most of it. It was used as an "opener" for the television program *20/20*. It was a 24-cel cycle that looked like the lights from a searchlight moving back and forth. It was used for a couple of years by the program.

I worked for Kurtz and Friends off and on, just like I did for other studios. By 1985, I had been in the business almost fifty years. In another year, I would have my twenty years with the Motion Picture Screen Cartoonists Union, and the 20,000 hours required for the complete health and welfare package. I needed only one more year and only 780 hours.

I was doing a lot of work for Kurtz and Friends and had high hopes that the work would last until I was eligible for retirement. Fate decreed otherwise. Kurtz and Friends suddenly went nonunion. I could have stayed there longer if I were interested just in a salary, but at this point in my life, it was necessary that I find work with a union shop.

The staff was faced with the loss of union benefits if we stayed on with the studio. In our ink and paint department, I was the only one to leave. Even though they didn't want to lose their union benefits, the other women needed their jobs, for our business was going through a very slow period.

All the girls were very concerned about me, especially Jan Cornell, my boss. She kept calling supervisors at other studios in my behalf. Time after time, Jan called Joan Orloff at Film Fair, and Joan replied that as soon as she had more work than her small staff could handle, she definitely would hire me.

Things were not the same anymore. Work was not as plentiful. I picked up some hours here and there from C & D Ink and Paint, Auril Thompson, and Fred Calvert, narrowing down the hours I needed to retire to 184, or just twenty-three days. One would think this would be a cinch. But it didn't work out that way.

It was now 1986, the year I had hoped to retire. Every week, I made the rounds of all the union shops. I even wrote a resumé, something I had never had to do in my entire career. But I couldn't give up when I was that close to the benefits that would give me a pension and medical coverage.

# [ *chapter 21* ]

# FILM FAIR

Would you believe that it took *two years* to get those twenty-three days! Finally, in October of 1988, Joan Orloff, ink and paint supervisor at Film Fair, hired me. She knew that I needed only twenty-three days more of work, but I told her I would work for her as long as she needed me.

They were working on an animated segment of Minnie Mouse, where she dances with Elton John in a live-action picture for Disney. The name of this special was "Totally Minnie."

During my time there, we worked on commercials for Keebler, Coors Beer, and others. After six months, Joan was kind enough to let me go, and I was ready. I was thrilled that, at my leaving, the people with whom I had worked presented me with a collage of characters we had worked on in those commercials. Each girl had autographed it. It is something I still prize very highly.

I really enjoyed working at Film Fair. Joan was such a good person to work for, and all the people there were also terrific. But I feel I had Jan Cornell to thank for recommending me so highly.

Several years later, Jan and her husband, John Mattias, retired. They now live in Julian, California, where they are so very much involved in community organizations, such as the Historical Society and Friends of the Library.

During March 2001, they were in the Los Angeles area. It was our pleasure to take them through the Warner Bros. Museum. I knew they would be interested, for Jan had worked at Warner Bros. for seven years.

I asked her how she got into the business. She told me she was working at MGM as a messenger and had a burning desire to get into the cartoon unit. Sometimes her job took her to that part of the studio, and she became fascinated with what they were doing.

She kept applying for a job as a painter, to no avail as they were hiring only experienced help at that time. But they put her on a mile-long waiting list.

She told all her friends about her frustrating situation. One of these friends was a member of a little musical group that got together once a week after their day jobs. It just so happened that the pianist was a Warner Bros. animator. His name? Virgil Ross! Virgil, being the wonderful and always helpful kind of guy, offered to tell the personnel manager about Jan. He would make an appointment for Jan, without even knowing her, and suggested that she take a few drawings with her to show what she could do.

Jan was so excited. Not only did she plan to take her art work with her, but when she told one of her acquaintances in the ink and paint department at MGM, this inker gave her some ink, paint, cels, and a bit of instruction on how to apply the paint. After practicing several days, Jan kept her appointment with Johnny Burton. He looked at the cels, and then changed the subject to other things. After a short while, he got up and they both started to leave his office. Jan finally got up the nerve and meekly asked, "Am I hired?" He replied, "Yes, of course." This began a long and fruitful career for Jan that started in the mid-1940s.

# chapter 22

# BILL MELENDEZ PRODUCTIONS

Bill Melendez has been a part of the cartoon business since the mid-1930s, when he started at Disney as an inbetweener. For the last forty years, he has been the head of his own studio, Bill Melendez Productions.

He came to Leon Schlesinger's as an assistant animator after the Disney strike in 1941. Bill was well liked by all of us, and because of his great skill and talent, he soon became an animator. He was part of the Bob Clampett, Art Davis, and Bob McKimson units.

Bill left Warner Bros. in 1948 and worked at United Productions of America (UPA), Sutherland's, and Play House Pictures before becoming associated with Charles Schulz of the Peanuts comic strip fame in 1964.

He formed his own company and, with Charles Schulz, produced "A Charlie Brown Christmas." This was such a tremendous hit on television that, each year, it has been shown so that new generations of kids can watch it.

The success of this joint venture led to many more Peanuts Gang specials and to commercials for Met Life (Metropolitan Life Insurance Co.).

Bill Melendez with Martha and Sol at the Fine Arts Gallery in Marina Del Rey, California, where cels and drawings from his studio were exhibited and sold. Photo by Michael Woolsey.

Bill located his studio on Larchmont Boulevard just south of Melrose Avenue in Los Angeles. What was so different about this studio was that it was comprised of three residential houses side-by-side. This may have contributed to the homey atmosphere that was felt by everyone working there. Plus, Bill's whole attitude toward his employees made for a very pleasant working environment.

When his studio was swamped with work and facing a deadline, he would farm out some of the work to Celine Miles Ink and Paint. This was at the time I was employed by Celine. It seems that we worked on all his specials, including "Yes, Virginia, There Is a Santa Claus." The Peanuts characters were easy to work on, with the exception of Woodstock, whose feathers gave us fits.

Many years after Celine Miles sold her business, I was able to pick up work directly from Melendez. Joanne Lansing was the head of ink and paint and an absolute gem to work for. (Joanne died in 1999, a tragic loss for all who knew her.) It was also good being reacquainted with friends I had worked with at other studios, Joan and Al Pabian, Olaya Stevenson, Jane Gonzales, and Roubina Janian. Another old-time friend, Colene Gonzales, also worked at home doing inking. There were times when Colene would ink a scene and then drop it off at my home for me to do the painting.

Melendez Productions was a great firm for me to work for, not only because I knew the boss from way back, but because everyone there seemed to really enjoy his or her job. Bill was the kind of producer who gave everyone involved screen credit.

The results of his work have garnered over twenty-five Emmy nominations, eight Emmys, an Oscar nomination, and many, many other awards.

Bill sold the houses on Larchmont in 1999 and relocated his studio in Sherman Oaks, California.

# [ *chapter 23* ]

# CENSORSHIP
# AND THE BLACK LIST

Way back in the early days of animation, we could have said, "anything goes." But in the 1930s, the Hays Office controlled the content
of feature films and animated cartoons with an iron fist. Once I was
in the story room at Schlesinger's when I noticed a typewritten page
with words and phrases tacked on the wall. I was shmoozing with
Mike Maltese and asked what that list was all about. He told me that
none of those words and phrases could be used in any of our cartoons,
in accordance with rulings by the Hays Office. The words, in themselves, were not necessarily risqué, but could have a double meaning.
That was not acceptable. I don't remember any of those words now,
but I am sure that all of them would pass inspection today.

Even though the directors and the story men were very careful,
some words and actions were still frowned upon. A couple of cartoons, by two different directors, Friz Freleng and Frank Tashlin,
released in the same month, September 1937, coincidentally, used
similar scenes. Frank's picture was "Speaking of the Weather," and
Friz's cartoon was "Dog Daze." Although both had different story
lines, one particular sequence was the same and caused quite a hul-
labaloo. This sequence was taken from a very popular movie series,

"The Thin Man," starring William Powell and Myrna Loy, both extremely popular in those days.

In one of those "Thin Man" detective pictures, William Powell is walking his dog Asta. Asta stops at a telephone pole to sniff. The Hays Office found nothing wrong with this. However, when it was used in Frank's cartoon, they censored it, we had to delete it, and we had to show that the dog didn't even go close to the pole. I suppose the censors wanted to shield children from seeing what a dog does naturally.

In "Dog Daze," we see people taking their dogs on leashes to a dog show. The arena looks like a regular movie theatre. A caricature of William Powell is walking his dog Asta and, as he gets toward the telephone pole, the next thing we see is a close-up of Powell with a knowing look on his face. The dog is not to be seen. This sequence was acceptable.

In *Look Magazine* in January 1939, there was an article published entitled "Hollywood Censors Its Animated Cartoons." Most of us at the studio saw it then, but it was long forgotten until one of my friends happened to mention it recently. So I called Jerry Beck, who I think knows just about everything about Warner Bros. cartoons. Sure enough, he had a copy of the article and sent me a xeroxed copy.

The cover shows Porky and Petunia Pig on a film strip holding hands. In the next frame, they are shown kissing on the lips. That was not o.k. with the Hays Office.

Also on the front page is a statement from Leon Schlesinger: "We cannot forget that while the cartoon today is excellent entertainment for young and old, it is primarily the favorite motion picture fare of children. Hence, we always must keep their best interests at heart by making our product proper for their impressionable minds."

The next four pages are photos and captions on censorable subjects used in cartoons from various studios.

Another outrageous thing the Hays Office meddled with was a Disney character. In a 1930 cartoon by Disney, Clarabell Cow only wore a "smile and a cow bell." No one objected to her udders showing. But, two years later, censors decreed that Clarabell had to wear a skirt. And further, in 1939, she would have to wear even more and walk upright. So, she wore a dress.

One of the strongest edicts from the Hays Office was that "crime must not pay." If there is a villian who commits a crime, he must get caught and go to jail.

While cartoons in the early days contained matter relative to religions, races, and politics in a negative way and were allowed by the Hays Office, these cartoons today are not permitted to be shown on television for they would be considered politically incorrect.

Much has been written about the "Black List" in the entertainment business. So many years have passed that I don't remember when it all started. I do know that it was after World War II and about the time the cold war started with the Soviet Republic.

In many cities across the United States, the House Un-American Activities Committee (HUAC) held hearings pertaining to communists and former communists in all parts of the entertainment industry. People who were subpoenaed could not defend themselves or explain their beliefs unless they gave the committee names of others they thought were communists. If a person admitted that he or she was a former member and refused to name names, he or she could be sent to prison for contempt of Congress. As a result, many people refused to give anything but their name and took the Fifth Amendment. Those that did this were "black listed" by the Motion Picture Alliance. This included people in animation.

The most ironic part of the Black List and these hearings came out in a book by Victor Navasky titled *Naming Names*. He reported that the Los Angeles Police Department Intelligence Division infiltrated the Communist Party starting in 1928. From 1936 to 1945, two Los Angeles police officers were the party's membership directors. FBI informants provided similar information from 1947 to 1949. The HUAC already had access to the Communist Party membership list and had, actually, no reason to gather names and information except to create a public spectacle that served the interests of the committee members. Ironically, the Communist Party, in those days, was a legal entity.

Charlotte Darling worked in the background department at Schlesinger's, but she spent a lot of time in the restroom smoking and trying to collect money for her causes. She tried having us sign petitions for one thing or another.

Gladys Hallberg, who was very outspoken, one day asked her point blank, "Charlotte, are you a communist?" Without hesitation, Charlotte answered, "Yes and I'm proud of it. It is a legal organization, you know, and we have no intentions of overthrowing the government like everybody thinks." A few other people chimed in on the discussion, including me. She did stop harassing people after that.

All this took place before World War II. So, you can imagine my surprise in 1953 when I read in the newspaper that Charlotte Darling Adams was a friendly witness to the House Un-American Committee and named many names. I am told that no one in the studio spoke to her after that.

Soon after, Charlotte left the studio, and I never worked with her again, but I ran into her from time to time and could never bring myself to bring up the subject.

The last time I saw her was in 1988 in Cairns, Australia, of all places. Sol and I had been in Australia visiting family and were awaiting our flight from Cairns to Honolulu. In Australia, it is necessary to purchase a departure stamp in order to leave the country. At that time, it was ten dollars per person. On his way back to where I was waiting for him, Sol encountered a bunch of young men and women who, we later found out, were from the United States and had been playing softball with various Australian teams. Who came at the end of all these young people but Charlotte Darling Huffine. Sol recognized her immediately but wasn't able to think of her name. She looked at him and, pointing her finger at him, she exclaimed, "Martha Goldman!" This jogged his memory and he replied, pointing his finger at her, "Charlotte Darling!"

She wanted to know my whereabouts and Sol brought her over to me. It turns out that the manager of that softball team was Michael Adams, Charlotte's son. Since there were young women members of that team, it was felt that a chaperone was needed, and Michael had asked his mother to fill in. What a small world!

The Black List lasted for many years and affected our first Screen Cartoon Guild as well as some of the individuals in the cartoon industry. The Guild we belonged to was not as powerful as the International Alliance of Theatrical Stage Employees (IATSE), which was the union for most of the studio crafts. In the early days, it was run by gangsters such as Willie Bioff and George Brown, both of whom were prosecuted by the government, found guilty, and sent to prison.

The head of the IATSE, after the departure of Bioff and Brown, was Roy Brewer, who was thought to be paranoid about communists in the union. So during the time of the Black List, he forced cartoon studios to fire suspected communists. These people sued and won since there never was any proof that they, indeed, were communists.

# chapter 24

# OTHER HAPPENINGS

## UNION BENEFITS

In the early 1950s, the IATSE had greater benefits to offer us, so the cartoonists in the big studios such as Disney, Warner's, and MGM voted to join. Some of the employees of the smaller studios were still covered by the guild. But, little by little, most of them joined the internal alliace. As far as I know, the only two that remained with the guild were Bill Melendez and Jay Ward.

I didn't join the IATSE until I joined Snowball, owned by Bob Clampett, in 1960. Since it was an IATSE studio, I needed to become a member. Although I was reluctant to join because of the past gangster domination, Roy Brewer no longer headed this union, and I was happy that I did join. The reason, of course, was the medical and retirement benefits. As far as I can remember, the salary scale was about the same.

In this new union, it took seven years before a member could be vested for retirement benefits, and each member had to work a minimum of four hundred hours a year. If one did not have the four hundred hours for two consecutive years, they lost all benefits and had to start over again. That happened to me because I did not keep track of my hours, only to find out too late that I was short just fifty hours in one year and just five hours in the second year. For full benefits, pension plus health and welfare, one needed twenty years as an IATSE member, with a minimum of twenty thousand hours.

## SCHLESINGER REUNION OF 1966

In 1966, our younger son, Lee, was going to have his bar mitzvah. Two of the people we invited were Helen Cope Berg and her husband, Percy, who lived in Everson, Washington. I had worked with Helen at Schlesinger's, and we were good friends. Upon receipt of our invitation, Helen wrote back, "As long as we're going to be in the Los Angeles area for a week, do you think we can get a few of the old gang together? It's been so long since I've seen them."

So I asked some of our old friends, people I knew were close to Helen and who would enjoy seeing her again. It started with just a half a dozen people, but, as the word got out, more and more people wanted to join us. We decided to make this a real reunion.

Dixie Smith and I coordinated the whole thing. I distributed fliers to all the studios calling the attention of all former Schlesinger employees to our reunion. We booked a private dining room at the Queens Arms Restaurant on Ventura Boulevard in Encino. Dixie handled the reservations list. Would you believe that 104 people showed up, including Chuck Jones, Tex Avery, Mel Blanc, Mike Maltese, Johnny Burton Sr., Herman Cohen, Norm and Fern McCabe, Bob McKimson, Auril and Dick Thompson, Raynelle Day, Sid Sutherland, Nelson Demerest, Jack Stevens, Dave and Shirley Kahn, Ruth Pierce Cavert, Dixie and Paul Smith, Enid Denbo Wizig, Leona Garber Hertzberg, and so many others?

We had such a wonderful time. It was great for all of us to be able to see and talk with the people we hadn't seen in so many years. We even received a telegram from Treg Brown, who, the night before, had received an Academy Award for the best sound for a feature motion picture entitled *The Great Race*. He expressed his sadness at not being able to be with us, for he had so many appointments for interviews with all the media. I personally was very disappointed, for he was now living in Spain and this would have been the golden opportunity for all of us to see and talk with him.

Messages also were received from Gil Turner and from Tedd Pierce, who were ill. Chuck Jones was master of ceremonies; Tex Avery spoke; Mel Blanc told us a bunch of his stories with his character accents. You can understand why we had such a good time.

## GOLDEN AWARD

In 1986, I received the Motion Picture Screen Cartoonists Golden Award for having been in the business for over fifty years. Having worked beyond those years, I finally retired in 1989. On the top of a nice wooden block is a small golden pegboard. On the face of it is this inscription: "Motion Picture Screen Cartoonists, Golden Award, Presented to MARTHA SIGALL, for 50 Years Service to the Craft, March 8, 1986."

## POST-RETIREMENT

Since retiring, authors, cartoon buffs, newspaper people, graduate students, college professors, and others have been interviewing me over the years. Probably the first of the professors was Don Crafton, who was the Theatre Arts Department head at the University of Wisconsin at Madison. Recently, we learned that he is now with Notre Dame University. The results of that interview appeared in an article he wrote for *Film History*, an international journal published in England. The article was titled "The View from Termite Terrace" and was later included in a book entitled *Reading the Rabbit*, edited by Kevin S. Sandler.

Karl Cohen quotes me in his book *Forbidden Animation*, which talks about animation people who were included in the Hollywood Black List of the House Un-American Committee. Karl called from his home in San Francisco to ask me questions about Charlotte Darling Huffine.

Another professor who visited me here at my home in Culver City was Gene Walz from the University of Winnepeg, Canada. He was here to collect information for a book he was writing on Charlie Thorsen, a character design artist, who I worked with at Schlesinger's. The title of his book is *Cartoon Charlie*.

I was also interviewed by Michael Barrier, who was then writing his book *Hollywood Cartoons*.

Fairly recently, Mike Mallory, an animation writer, called to tell me that he was writing an article for the *Los Angeles Times* Calendar Section entitled "Move Over, Old Men." He was writing about women in animation today and wanted someone from the past as well, so he included me.

Back in 1995, upon recommendation of Jerry Beck, a production company out of Wilmington, Delaware, Teleduction Associates, Inc., headed by Sharon Baker, contacted me for an interview to be used in a television documentary entitled "Cartoons Go to War." The company was preparing the film since that year was the fiftieth anniversary of the end of World War II. The interview was conducted here in our home at the end of May.

You should have seen my studio work room. They had cables running all over the floors, lights and reflectors, a monitor so they could watch what they were taping, and so on. They even brought a make-up woman with them.

I wasn't the only one in this film. Included were Chuck Jones, Mark Kausler, Jerry Beck, Mike Glad, Michael Shull, and David Wilt, the last two being professors at Maryland University and authors of a book entitled *Doing Their Bit*, which covered "Wartime American Animated Short Films, 1939–1945."

This documentary was aired on the Arts and Entertainment channel on August 31, 1995. It has been shown many times across the country and internationally. It has also been shown, from time to time, on the History Channel. Just recently, I received an e-mail message from a cousin now living in Israel. Would you believe, she recognized my voice before even seeing the picture on television!

Coincidentally, I'm mentioned in Shull and Wilt's book, too, with reference to a film short called "Point Rationing of Food." This six-minute black-and-white cartoon was produced by the Leon Schlesinger studio, which had been asked by the Screen Cartoonists Guild to produce it, directed by Chuck Jones. It was prepared for the Office of Price Administration by forty members of Local 852, Screen Cartoonists, over a three-week period of evenings and weekends. Its purpose was to explain to the general public how to use their ration books wisely so that their stamps would last from month to month. Our time was donated, none of us got paid.

You must remember, this was wartime and ration stamps were issued to everyone in the country for such items as coffee, sugar, butter, meats, and gasoline. This short was devoted to just the food items.

In 1997, I was asked by Tom Sito, the vice president of ASIFA, to be interviewed by him at an ASIFA meeting. I was asked about how I got into the business, and I told some of the stories I've related here. A question-and-answer period followed. One of the best parts of the evening was that it gave me the opportunity to make some new friends.

A woman asked if I would object to her taping the conversation. At the end of the session, she even took a couple of photos. I didn't know it at the time, but this woman was Maureen Furniss, an instructor at Chapman University, Film and Television Department, who subsequently had a book published entitled *Art in Motion—Animation Aesthetics*, which included a picture she had taken of me with a short description of my ASIFA interview. Among the other people in the business I met that night were Bill Perkins and Rhonda Hicks, from Warner Bros. Feature Animation, and Tom Klein, animator/animation supervisor for Knowledge Adventure, Inc., in Glendale.

In February 2000, a production company out of New York headed by Greg Ford with Margaret Selby as producer/director came to southern California to do a documentary tribute to Chuck Jones which they titled "Chuck Jones: Extremes and In-Betweens, A Life in Animation." Many people well known in feature films and animation were part of taped interviews for this project.

Their names as listed in the program are:

| | | |
|---|---|---|
| Ken Burns | Ron Howard | Lorne Michaels |
| Joe Dante | Marian Jones | Rob Minkoff |
| Roger Ebert | Richard Jones | Maurice Noble |
| June Foray | Linda Jones-Clough | Andre Previn |
| Stan Freberg | Norton Juster | John Schulman |
| Bob Givens | Glen Keane | Martha Sigall |
| Eric Goldberg | John Lasseter | Steven Spielberg |
| Whoopi Goldberg | Leonard Maltin | Robin Williams |
| Matt Groening | Roger Mayer | |

On Thursday, September 21, 2000, Chuck's eighty-eighth birthday, this program had its premiere in the Steven J. Ross Theatre on the Warner Bros. lot. At least three to four hundred people attended. It was a real gala evening. Sol and I enjoyed it tremendously.

The TV presentation of this film took place on November 22, 2000, on local Public Broadcasting stations all over the country as part of PBS's *Great Performances*.

On October 22, 2003, the Academy of Motion Picture Arts and Sciences and the Academy Foundation presented a program produced by Randy Haberkamp entitled "Animation at War." Featured were five short World War II cartoons: "Song of Victory" (Columbia, 1943), "Out of the Frying Pan into the Firing Line" (Disney, 1942), "Reason and Emotion" (Disney, Oscar Nominee 1943), "Russian Rhapsody" (Warner Bros., 1943), and "Blitz Wolf" (MGM, Oscar Nominee 1942.)

These were followed by a part-animation, part-documentary feature "Victory through Air Power" (Disney, 1943). This was based on Alexander P. de Seversky's 1942 book and utilized spectacular special effects, historical events, and humorous animation.

After the showing of these films, Jerry Beck moderated a panel consisting of David Bossert, a twenty-year veteran of Walt Disney Feature Animation, Leonard Maltin, a most respected film historian and critic, and me. We talked about the films that were shown and I spoke about my experiences during World War II, including the

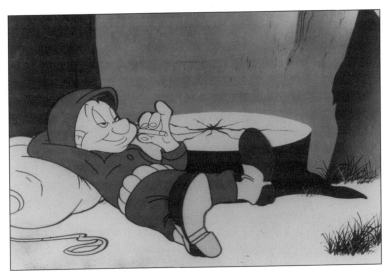

Pvt. Snafu. © Warner Bros. Entertainment, Inc. Courtesy of Jerry Beck.

Bugs Bunny in "Herr Meets Hare." © Warner Bros. Entertainment, Inc. Courtesy of Jerry Beck.

training films I had worked on such as "Private Snafu" for the United States Army while I was working for Leon Schlesinger Productions and technical training films for the United States Navy while I was at Graphic Films.

A question and answer period followed the panel discussion. The program was well received by the large audience.

When most people have a career in a business or profession and it's time to retire, they are usually through with anything related to their career. That's the way it had been for my family and friends, whether they were in animation or other fields, so why not me? I think one reason is that way, way back, as an apprentice painter, I fell in love with animated cartoons and the people who made them, and I never got over it. Another reason is that my husband, Sol, wouldn't let me. As one who did not work in the business, he was actually more fascinated than I.

Then Robert Patrick entered my life, and I embarked on a new and exciting adventure. One day, when Sol and I were visiting at Linda Jones Enterprises in Irvine, California, we were introduced to Robert, whose position with the firm is to place the animation art of Chuck Jones into galleries all over the world.

He asked me, if he were able to arrange it, would I be willing to make an appearance at any of these galleries and speak to invited guests regarding my years in animation and the cartoons that Chuck directed. He said that all of our expenses would be paid and would include an honorarium. I had never done anything like this before, so I told him I would think about it. I didn't have to think long.

Several weeks later, he called to say that he had arranged with Stage Nine Entertainment Store in Old Town Sacramento, California, to hold such an event. It was decided that on Friday night, November 7, the store would host an invitation only party for its best customers from 7 P.M. to 10 P.M. On the following day, Saturday, the store would be open to tourists and others walking by. The public was made aware of my presence on Saturday by a newspaper article in the *Sacramento Bee* and by large posters placed at the two entrances to the store.

Linda Jones Enterprises produced framed limited edition cels from the cartoon "Old Glory," which was released in 1939. I had worked on this picture, directed by Chuck Jones. These were offered for sale to the public.

I talked about everything I remembered about the cartoon plus other bits of animation information. People in attendance were very enthused and asked a lot of questions about all aspects of the cartoon business. Troy Carlson, owner of Stage Nine, remarked to me later that the weekend was a very successful one.

Stage Nine Entertainment is in the heart of Old Town Sacramento and not only handles animation art, but also displays all kinds of movie and animation memorabilia for sale. It seemed to me that they had thousands of items to satisfy every customer.

Sol and I enjoyed this weekend much more than we could have anticipated. Robert was very pleased and hopeful about doing something similar in other galleries.

Rain had been predicted for that entire weekend in Sacramento but, luckily, it held off until Saturday's event was over and then the skies just opened up. Sol, for years, has called me a "weather witch." He credits me for using my "powers" to hold off the rain during my appearances.

## WARNER BROS. MUSEUM

In June of 1996, Warner Bros. opened a museum on their lot in Burbank. They were the first movie studio to have such a museum available to the public. The night it opened was a gala affair attended by notable movie and animation people and their families. There were more than five hundred people there to see how and what Warner Bros. had done to exhibit their movie and animation memorabilia.

About fifty Warner Bros. retirees and Sol and I had been trained for several months to be docents. Don Foster, Gene Marks, and I were the only ones who had had experience in animation. Even though Sol had never worked in the studio, he and other spouses were welcomed as docents, too.

It was just about closing time on that first exciting evening when a beautiful young woman came up the stairs to view the animation.

Martha and Sol at the Warner Bros. Museum. © Warner Bros. Entertainment, Inc.

Martha and Don Foster. © Warner Bros. Entertainment, Inc.

Sol, Carla Hanawalt, Pat Kowalski, and Leith Adams. © Warner Bros. Entertainment, Inc.

Sol and Lisa Janney with kids. © Warner Bros. Entertainment, Inc.

The first thing a visitor would see was a painted picture with the faces of Tex Avery, Chuck Jones, Carl Stalling, Mel Blanc, Bob Clampett, Friz Freleng, and Bob McKimson. Added to their shoulders and heads were the cartoon characters they made famous.

This young lady just stood looking at this picture for several moments. I went over to her, and since I knew and worked with all of these men, I asked her if she had any questions regarding these people. She told me she was just looking at her grandfather. I asked which one he might be. When she told me, "Bob McKimson," I said, "I knew him for many years." Her reply was, "Won't you please tell me everything you know about him, for I was only six years old when he died."

As I told her all I knew about what a talented man he was, we both cried and hugged each other. She was so grateful to be able to talk with someone who had worked with him.

I have thought of that darling girl often since that night and what a terrible loss his death was to his family. But how lucky it was for so many of us who had the privilege of knowing him.

Sol remembers best the afternoon we had two film crews come by, one from Venezuela and the other from South Korea, each with an interpreter since none of the others spoke English. Included in the Venezuela group were two beautiful movie actresses.

At the back of the room, there were four caricatures of movie stars that I had inked and painted for our friends, Joey and John Norin, who loaned them to the museum. John is the manager of the make-up department at Warner Bros. When Sol explained to the interpreter of the Venezuelan group, the first of the two groups to come through, that the caricatures had been made by his wife, they all got excited when his words were translated to the other members of the group. They asked immediately if I was there that afternoon. He brought them over to me, and they interviewed and taped my description of how cartoons were made. They asked many questions and seemed to have a great time.

About an hour later, a South Korean group came through with their interpreter, and the same thing was repeated.

This is so fresh in Sol's mind for, although he didn't think of it at the time, he felt he should have asked each group for a copy of the tape when they returned home. In Venezuela, they speak Spanish. In Korea, it's Korean. They couldn't possibly air my English conversation. It would either have to be dubbed into the language of their home country or they would have to use subtitles. He thought that if they had used the former method, wouldn't it have been great to see and hear me speaking Spanish and Korean?

Being docents has been a wonderful, interesting, and rewarding experience for the both of us. It has given us the opportunity to meet and talk with people from all over the world. The head archivist of the museum, Leith Adams, and his assistant, Pat Kowalski, the people we have the most direct contact with, are so knowledgeable, friendly, and cooperative. There are over fifty other docents who volunteer their time, and we have enjoyed working with them as well.

## OUR CARTOON GROUP

When Sol and I were married, I had a whole group of friends from animation who naturally became his friends, too. He would refer to them as our "cartoon group" for either the husband or wife or both of them worked in animation.

Every few months, we would all get together at someone's home or we would go out to dinner. Sol found out, way back then, that you couldn't get as few as even just two people from animation together in the same room where they didn't immediately, and I mean immediately, start reminiscing. He has always felt that the stories they told were priceless. Some of those stories, especially those told by Mike Maltese, were hilarious and Sol would be holding his stomach, he was laughing so hard.

For years, especially as some of those friends began to pass on, Sol had wanted to preserve those stories for future generations. Unfortunately, in the beginning, we didn't have the wherewithal for the necessary equipment. Camcorders weren't even available at that time.

The small personal movie cameras didn't record sound. And what about the necessary lighting?

A couple of years ago, we approached a vice president at Warner Bros. whom we had met through the museum about Warner Bros. backing us with the needed equipment. She was told they would do so, but wanted us to limit the taping to just former Warner employees. This we couldn't do, for these stories originated in so many other studios as well.

It wasn't until we attended a luncheon meeting of the group Women in Animation, of which I am a member and their first honoree, and mentioned this to one of its members, Kellie-Bea Rainey (now Cooper), that we got the response we had looked for for so long, "Let's do it." She had a large camcorder, borrowed lights from a friend, and we were off! I have had contact with some of my buddies from the old days and I started lining up appointments with them for taping. Some have come to our home. Where the person was physically unable to do so, we went to their home. So far, we have taped nineteen of them and we are trying to set up dates for others. After our first three or four sessions, Judy Rauh (now Simmons) joined us and became one of the team. Judy works in postproduction in television. Kellie-Bea has a number of years in animation behind her and all of us are thoroughly enjoying the stories we have heard from these "old-timers."

In doing this, we have tried to pair at least two people together for we have found that they play off each other. One will say something that will remind the other of something else, and so on, back and forth. In one instance, we have interviewed three together. At another time, we had just one person. When there is a lull in the conversation, either I or Sol or Kellie-Bea would interject, from off-camera, with a question to get them started again.

When we are all finished, and have no others left to tape, it is our intention to give copies of these tapes to schools, colleges, and universities that teach animation. This hasn't all been worked out yet, for we are devoting all our available time to taping as many people as we possibly can. But we have become even more convinced that these stories should not be lost, that they should be handed down from generation to generation.

# LOONEY TUNES: GOLDEN COLLECTION

Jerry Beck informed me that Warner Bros. was producing a DVD set of fifty-six classic Warner Bros. cartoons. He was asked to be a consultant on the project to be produced by New Wave Entertainment. Included in these cartoons would be commentaries by some of the people who worked on these cartoons. He suggested I participate in the project. He had already given my name to Constantine Nasr, who was in charge of the interviewing.

Constantine did call and ask if I could be filmed on Thursday, April 24, at 1 P.M. When I agreed, he said that several others, and he named them, also were scheduled for the same day and time, that they had decided to meet for lunch at an Alcapulco Restaurant near the studio in Burbank. The only person I knew of this group was Art Leonardi. I had enough experience to know that cartoon people are all of the same breed, so I welcomed the invitation.

The group consisted of Willie Ito and Bob Singer, both of whom I had met just once, and Margaret Nichols and Corny Cole, both of whom I had never met. Sol and I made up the seven of us who met for lunch.

As usual, Art had his digital camcorder with him and recorded the entire session. As always happens when cartoonists get together, the stories and the laughter never ended. None of us really finished our lunch for we were laughing so hard so much of the time. Our eating and laughter stopped only because New Wave Entertainment called the restaurant and asked them to tell us interviewing time had arrived. Upon arrival at New Wave, we were put into a conference room where the hilarity continued.

Jerry Beck joined us and we were shown one of the cartoons to be used in the set, "Baseball Bugs." The quality was so much better than the original print and we were told that all of the cartoons to be used would be so enchanced.

About 2 P.M., Lisa Gilmore, a production associate on the project, introduced herself and asked which one of us would prefer to go first. It was decided that the one who had the greatest distance to travel should be that person. Bob Singer, who lives in Orange County, about fifty or sixty miles from New Wave, went first. When he finished, he came back into our room and rejoined the group—and the stories continued.

Willie Ito went second and he then returned to the group—and more stories.

Willie was followed by Art Leonardi, who was followed by Margaret Nichols, who was followed by me. As each of us returned to the conference room, we found the stories were still in full swing.

All of the stories were so funny, we held our stomachs all afternoon. One of the funniest ones was told by Corny, who is now a teacher at Cal Arts, a very prestigous art school that includes animation in its curriculum. He said that when he was getting started in the business, he burned the midnight oil having fun. When he came to work, he would be so sleepy.

As you may know, the animation is drawn over a lightboard. The animators would have at least three drawings on their pegboard at a time and would use their fingers on the hand that didn't hold the pencil to flip the drawings back and forth to insure that the movement was correct.

Corny said that he figured out a way to hold his pencil in one hand while he flipped the drawings with the fingers of the other—while he slept. When his supervisor would look at him, he wouldn't notice that he was sleeping, for his fingers were moving! How he maintained his footage quota, he didn't say.

## CARTOONS WERE MADE TO ENTERTAIN

I have heard many directors and writers say that they made cartoons for themselves. If they thought they were funny, they believed the movie-going audiences would also think they were funny. Cartoons were not made for kids, but no one told that to kids, because they really loved them. Many grown men have told me that animated cartoons had a great affect on their lives, that these cartoons shaped their sense of humor.

Time constraints put a lot of pressure on the creative directors and writers in animation. They would be expected to come up with a new story idea and complete the storyboard in about six weeks. Luckily, cartoons were very contemporary and, at times, reflected whatever was going on in the world. Famous people and, especially, movie stars, became fair game for the story men. For example, they would incorporate things the stars had said that the public picked up on. Comedians Red Skelton, Jerry Colonna, the Marx Brothers, and others would crop up into these cartoons from time to time.

Even the Hays Office was lampooned, in "A Tale of Two Kitties." It stars two cats, Babbit and Catstello, a takeoff on the comedy team of years ago, Abbott and Costello. Babbit says, "Give me the bird, give me the bird." Catstello's reply, "If the Hays Office would only let me, I'd give 'im the bird all right."

Anything of interest to society was sure to be used in a cartoon. The prime purpose of these creative people was to earn a livelihood, to support their families. The more popular their cartoons, the faster they would advance in their craft.

Years ago, the theatres, in order to secure a feature film, had to take a newsreel and a cartoon, as well. This practice was referred to as "block booking." Theatre owners actually went to court to rescind this practice, and they won. The result was that cartoons were no longer booked in all the theatres. As a result, there were mass layoffs in the animation industry.

Luckily for our business, in a relatively short time, television was beginning to take hold. The existing animation studios had a resurgence of production. New studios like Hanna-Barbera, DePatie-Freleng, Filmation, and lots of independents sprang up, along with a few ink and paint services.

Television was a boon to the cartoon business in other respects, for television used cartoons extensively. The children of that generation, like our sons, Bob and Lee, and millions of other kids grew up watching not only the new cartoons being generated, but those of the early years as well. It was from this generation that we now have a multitude of cartoon buffs, historians, and others at all levels within the industry. It is these people who regard the 1930s, the 1940s, and the 1950s as the "Golden Age of Animation." This may be true, but we surely didn't recognize it at the time. But, speaking for the remaining old-timers, we now heartily agree.

Today, there are schools that teach every phase of animation. Colleges and universities now teach film and animation history. I hope they all don't teach it the way some of these professors write about it. They dissect and psychoanalyze the motives of the creators as if they had a hidden agenda. It seems that these teachers never mention the humor, which is what these cartoons are all about—making people laugh.

## IF THESE WALLS COULD TALK!

I have mentioned stories and other things that happened at the studios I worked for. But I certainly was not privy to everything that went on. And many things that happened I have long forgotten. In my fifty-three-plus-year career, I worked for a total of twenty-four different studios. My tenure at each of them ranged from a couple of weeks to seven years, with my on-and-off freelance at Celine Miles covering a period of twenty-five years!

What happened at all the other studios that I didn't work for? Wouldn't it be great if ALL the scene planning, gag writing, and pranks the people played on each other could be known to us?

At least five companies occupied that building at 861 North Seward at Willoughby Avenue in Hollywood. I heard that it was initially the location for a lab that processed film for "Steamboat Willie."

During the time that Harman-Ising produced "Merrie Melodies and Looney Tunes" for Leon Schlesinger, they were located in a little building at 5653 Hollywood Boulevard near Wilton Place. When they broke with Schlesinger, they moved to the 861 North Seward address.

Next to occupy the Seward address building was the "Bambi" unit from Disney, which was there until that picture was finished.

Still giving no rest to 861 North Seward, Screen Gems, a studio owned by Columbia Pictures, moved in. They were formerly with Mintz, located at 7000 Santa Monica Boulevard at Orange Avenue. Screen Gems called it quits in the late 1940s. But it wasn't long before

Harman-Ising Studio, Hollywood Boulevard, near Wilton, 1930–33.

Ub Iwerks Studio, 9713 Santa Monica Boulevard, Beverly Hills, 1933–36.

Charles Mintz Studio, Santa Monica Boulevard, at Orange, Hollywood.

Charles Mintz Studio, Santa Monica Boulevard.

Entrance to 861
Seward, Hollywood.

861 Seward, Hollywood: Disney lab for "Steamboat
Willie"; Harman-Ising; Disney's "Bambi" unit; Screen
Gems; Walter Lantz; Abe Levitow.

Walter Lantz moved his studio to this address. Lantz rented out the upper floor to Abe Levitow, who was producing commercials.

Can you imagine all the things those walls would have to say?

Harman-Ising, in 1929, made the test film "Bosko, the Talk-Ink Kid" in the Otto K. Olson building on Vine Street at Selma Avenue. In addition to Rudy and Hugh, others who worked on this test included Friz Freleng, Paul Smith, C. G. Maxwell, Ham Hamilton, and Ray Abrams. C. G. Maxwell did the voice of Bosko. Ham Hamilton's sister played the piano. They made this three-minute pilot after becoming displaced persons from the short-lived, unsuccessful Winkler Studio at 1154 North Western Avenue in Hollywood.

The pilot was shopped around throughout the business, both on the West Coast as well as on the East Coast, looking for a producer. It was Leon Schlesinger who finally gave it the "go ahead."

During World War II, United Productions of America started a studio at the Otto K. Olson building. My first introduction to that studio was when I volunteered to finish "Hell Bent for Election." In order to get into this building, we had to climb the stairs to the roof of the building next door and cross a bridge that was built to enable us to get into the Olson building. I wish I could remember why such a procedure was necessary.

I did this routine for several months when I went to work for UPA after the war was over. None of us thought that this was dangerous. In fact, we got a kick out of it. Now that I look back, we were lucky that that building next door didn't have a fire or some other disaster. How would we have gotten out?

What about the stories this building might tell?

The walls at Leon Schlesinger Productions certainly must have much to say. When I started at Schlesinger's, they were located at 1351 North Van Ness in Hollywood. That was the southwest end of the original Warner Bros. studio. At first, Schlesinger occupied a building on the north end, near Sunset Boulevard in Hollywood. This was right after Harman-Ising left.

When Tex Avery was hired as a director in 1935, he was given a small studio in the middle of the lot, which was the real Termite Terrace. Chuck Jones, Bob Clampett, Virgil Ross, Sid Sutherland, and Bobo Cannon were all animators in this unit.

In the summer of 1936, Schlesinger decided to combine all the units at 1351 North Van Ness. In 1939, the original building that was occupied by the Schlesinger Studio from 1933 to 1936 was remodeled and moved into by the "Katz unit." Ray Katz was in charge, and Bob Clampett was the director of this unit, which produced black-and-white Porky Pig cartoons.

In 1941, the studio at 1351 Van Ness was remodeled, and the Katz unit was brought back to that location. Before the remodeling, the ink and paint department consisted of forty girls and was located on the second floor. Upon completion of the remodeling, we were moved to the first floor, and there were then sixty of us.

The girls in the Katz unit never really considered themselves part of the Schlesinger studio. There was a lot of skepticism on the part of all the girls as to whether or not they would be able to get along with one another. After we got to know one another, we got along fine. Up until that point, those walls must have been reverberating with all kinds of "catty" remarks. Or, should I say, "K(for Katz)a-t-z-y remarks?"

Just imagine what the walls at the Walt Disney studio could tell us. The original location was at Hollywood Boulevard and Vermont Avenue while awaiting completion of the studio at Hyperion and Griffith Park Boulevard. It was the Hyperion location that produced the Mickey Mouse series, the "Donald Duck" series, the "Three Little Pigs," and "Snow White." In the late 1930s, Disney relocated to its current location at Buena Vista and Alameda in Burbank, California.

After Ub Iwerks left Disney in 1935, he opened a studio in Beverly Hills at 9713 Santa Monica Boulevard. Quite a few of the Disney people went with him, including Carl Stalling.

Hugh Harman left MGM sometime in 1940. His studio was located at 9122 Sunset Boulevard. Not too long after that, Rudy Ising became Major Ising of the U.S. Air Force and headed the first animation unit at Fort Roach in Culver City, where many of our animated cartoonists served in the armed forces during World War II.

I've mentioned gags and high-jinks that went on at the studios I worked at, but, most assuredly, these things happened in all the studios. If only these walls could talk!

# THE ANNIE AWARDS

The highlight of these retirement years occurred on Saturday, February 7, 2004. It was a weekend that Sol and I will never forget. Let me explain: almost everyone is familiar with the Oscar Awards presented every year by the Academy of Motion Pictures Arts and Sciences to those who have excelled in film that year, but there is also an international animation organization with a chapter in Los Angeles called ASIFA that recognizes those in animation who have excelled in this field.

As the Academy has its Oscar night, ASIFA has its Annie Awards night. This year, it was held at the Alex Theatre in Glendale, California, on February 7. As with the Academy, ASIFA, too, has numerous categories for which their awards are given.

Since the June Foray Award was not a contested category, only one person was nominated, and that person was me, Martha Sigall. Michael Mallory, a member of the selection committee, had written a letter to the committee recommending me for the award. I was told that there was almost instant agreement among the members.

Jerry Beck, one of the members of the committee, was asked by the others to call me with this wonderful surprise. I just couldn't believe it when he informed me I was to receive the June Foray Award! I was so excited. June Foray is the founding member of ASIFA, Hollywood. She is a voice actress who has done the voices of Rocky, the Flying Squirrel, and Natasha in the "Rocky and Bullwinkle Show." She also was Witch Hazel and Granny in the Warner Bros. cartoons. She was Cindy Lou in the "Grinch That Stole Christmas." There were many other Foray voices along the way.

What a wonderful thing to happen to me, a person who got so much pleasure and enjoyment from doing all things connected with animation. It was my life. It had been my life for over fifty-three years.

The author makes an acceptance speech after being presented with the ASIFA Hollywood June Foray Annie Award, February 7, 2004, at the Alex Theatre, Glendale, California. June Foray stands at right. Photo by Bob Sigall.

And, now, to receive such a prestigious award for doing the things I enjoyed doing so much, it was beyond my belief! To me, this was the highest recognition that could be given to any inker or painter.

Michael Mallory was also responsible for my biography printed in the program for that night. It reads as follows:

### JUNE FORAY AWARD
*Martha Sigall*

Martha Sigall's career in animation began in 1936 when she joined the ink and paint department at the Leon Schlesinger Studio, a.k.a. Termite Terrace. Working with the likes of Tex Avery, Bob Clampett, and Chuck Jones, she contributed to many seminal Looney Tunes and Merrie Melodies and witnessed the development of such classic characters as Bugs Bunny. In 1943, Martha moved to Graphic Films and spent the remainder of the War as a camera assistant. Leaving Graphic Films in 1945, she worked for a who's who list of animation studios, including UPA, MGM, Celine Miles Ink and Paint, Hanna-Barbera, Snowball, Grantray Lawrence, Depatie-Freleng, Murakami-Wolf, Fred Calvert, Kurtz and Friends, Film Fair and Bill Melendez—often freelancing while she raised her children.

Martha officially retired in 1989, but soon found herself busier than ever with volunteer work. She helped friends obtain video copies of their old cartoons and then took steps to make certain that the history of the American cartoon was recorded by interviewing and videotaping veterans. Starting in 1996, Martha became a volunteer docent for the Warner Bros. Museum educating visitors from around the globe about the studio and its legendary animation department. She has also shared her vast personal knowledge of the cartoon industry with an ever-growing audience through personal appearances and filmed interviews.

No animation writer, historian, researcher, documentarian, or fan is turned away from the home Martha shares with her husband, Sol, and all leave with a far greater understanding of what the Golden Age of cartoons was really like. Through her unfailing generosity, dedication to the medium, and ever-present good cheer, Martha Sigall is not only a valuable and vibrant member of the animation community at large, she is one of its greatest treasures.

What a thrill!

This wonderful feeling was greatly enhanced by the fact that our older son, Bob, and his wife, Lei, came from their home in Hawaii; our younger son, Lee, his wife, Eve, our granddaughter, Nicole, our grandson, Dustin, and Eve's parents, Jonni and Victor Mann, were all in attendance from San Diego. Having all these family members and our two close friends Jonni and Vic, and more friends Bronwen Barry and Kate and Emerson Johnson, in the theatre for this auspicious time was so wonderful for me. Lee and his family had to return to San Diego the following day. Bob and Lei were here until Monday. What a great event to bring the whole family together.

There was more—upon completion of June's introduction of me, I joined her on the stage from backstage where I had been waiting. Upon my entry, there was applause. Then, a lot more applause followed by a standing ovation from the whole audience. I couldn't believe what I was seeing and hearing. In my lifetime, I have never been honored in such a manner.

Four weeks later, I was given another surprise. The vice mayor of Culver City presented me with a City of Culver City Commendation which, after seven WHEREAS's, concluded with "NOW, THEREFORE, BE IT RESOLVED, that the City Council of the City of Culver City,

California hereby congratulates Martha Sigall for her selection as the recipient of the June Foray Award and thanks her for continuing to share her experiences with the students of Culver City. Dated this 8th Day of March, 2004, and signed by Steven Rose, Vice-Mayor."

On March 11, 2004, I was interviewed at home by Nancy Forrest, a reporter for the *Culver City News,* about my years in animation and my Annie Award. Her newspaper article appeared in the next week's Thursday edition.

## WILL IT EVER END?

In 1989, after more than fifty-three years in animation, I was able to retire, but, every now and then, I still get the urge to ink and paint cels. And I do this for family and friends. Painting cartoons is still so much a part of me that as long as I have a steady hand, a strong back, and my eyes hold out, I plan to continue putting color on cels and "living life inside the lines."

# [ *index* ]